Prepper's: The Ultimate Guide

Tadhg O'Flaherty

ISBN-13: 978-1-52053-652-1

To the entire human race.

Because you deserve to survive.

Table of Contents

WARNING

The survival techniques described in this book are only to be used during an actual apocalyptic style disaster, where the safety and future survival of you, your family or friends is at immediate risk. The author does not accept any responsibility for the use or misuse of any material contained in this book. The author is not a certified survival expert or medical doctor and the information contained in this book is not a guarantee of safety or survival.

In some countries, it may be illegal for a citizen to own a firearm or other weapon. Some techniques described may be deemed undesirable by society in general and may also be illegal depending on where you live. Some of these survival techniques may result in injury or death. If you decide to practise any of these survival techniques before a disaster then you do so at your own risk. Always consult a competent professional before practising any of the survival or medical techniques described.

Before acquiring or constructing any weapons or booby traps consult a competent legal professional.

Introduction

"It happened that a fire broke out backstage in a theatre. The clown came out to inform the public. They thought it was jest and applauded. He repeated his warning. They shouted even louder. So I think the world will come to an end amid the general applause from all the wits who believe that it is a joke."
Søren Kierkegaard (1813-1855)

You wake up to a typical summer's morning in Upper Manhattan and get yourself ready for another busy day at work. As you leave your apartment you see that things are a bit quiet and you have a feeling it's going to be a wonderful and productive day. The subway is going to be less busy and maybe you will get a place to sit... finally.

As you enter the train to discover that there are plenty of empty seats you thank your lucky stars and relax into your short commute. The train stops and you emerge from Wall Street subway station onto a sunny Broadway and take a few minutes to admire Trinity Church before making your way to work. It's interesting that you have emerged from this subway station a thousand times before but only on this quiet morning do you finally get the chance to admire this beautiful piece of architecture.

You treat yourself to a coffee and slowly make your way to work when suddenly a blinding flash of light from the North East grabs your attention. For a split second everything is deathly quiet, and then suddenly the air is shattered with a deafening roar. You are thrown backwards with such force that you black out for what seems an eternity.

As you begin to come round you realise something catastrophic has just happened. You can see destroyed buildings everywhere and the air is thick with a black dust that burns your eyes. All the windows as far as the eye can see are gone and the ground is littered with pieces of broken glass. As a small pulse of pain in your neck begins to develop into excruciating agony you reach up and realise that there is a large piece of glass sticking out of your neck. You decide to leave it there for now as you try to figure out what has happened to your beloved Manhattan.

Just when you thought things couldn't possibly get worse you see a wall of flames approaching very fast. You run as fast as you can, back to Wall Street subway station and just about manage to crawl through the mound of debris that is now blocking the entrance. As you join the masses of frightened people gathered there you overhear a soldier telling a policeman that New York was hit by a nuclear weapon. You can't believe what you are hearing. Over the screams of anguish and pain from your fellow survivors, you overhear snippets of the conversation; *"... Confirmed. LaGuardia ..."*, *"...800 kiloton yield based on damage estimates ..."*.

As you take this all in you realise that LaGuardia Airport is about 15km (9.5 miles) away. How could a nuke cause damage so far away? How am I going to get off the island? Everything I own has been destroyed. Who is going to help me?

In this realistic portrayal of a nuclear attack, LaGuardia Airport in New York was hit by a Russian-made Topol (SS-25) nuclear warhead with a yield of 800 kilotons. The initial fireball from the blast was 1km (0.6 miles) in diameter which completely vaporised everything within this range. This would be enough to completely destroy the runways, terminals and hangars at the airport. People will be able to see the blast from as far away as 30km (18.5 miles).

Further destruction was caused by the blast which was approximately 6.5km (4 miles) in diameter and big enough to reach buildings on Manhattan Island. This blast wave is powerful enough to completely destroy buildings, even those made from reinforced concrete or steel beam skyscrapers. Both the RFK Triborough Bridge and the Queensboro Bridge have been completely destroyed along with every building on Roosevelt Island. Vast areas of Brooklyn have been simply wiped off the map. Within this distance of the epicentre, most people have been killed with a small amount of badly injured survivors.

Further destruction is caused by thermal radiation (a wall of fire) that stretches to 11km (6.8 miles) from the epicentre. This fireball will immediately set anything on fire that it encounters. If you are within this area expect to receive a severe 3rd-degree burn, that's if you survive. This fireball of destruction will reach as far as our protagonist on Wall Street and will cause almost every building and person on

Manhattan Island to catch fire. At the time of writing, the population of Manhattan is 1.6 million. Approximately 95% of these will be either killed or so badly injured that they will be unable to help themselves and require emergency assistance. This does not include the casualties in Brooklyn or other affected areas.

This scenario is highly likely and it is very probable that a nuclear weapon of this yield is pointing directly at either LaGuardia airport or Manhattan itself.

In this book I will look at the following popular disasters that preppers are actively preparing for:

- Nuclear War
- Economic Collapse
- Super Volcano
- Asteroid Strike
- Chemical / Biological Warfare
- Global Tsunami
- Planet X
- Solar Flare / EMP
- Global Quake
- Pandemic
- Global Famine
- Alien Invasion

Regardless of how a catastrophic disaster may begin it is vital for you to prepare **now**. It will be too late once the apocalyptic events unfold. You will, most likely, not receive any form of warning if a nuclear war begins or if Planet X makes its way into our Solar System.

If you are new to prepping it's no different to packing for an extended holiday. The things you need to do for prepping are almost the same; make a list, get enough supplies, efficiently order your supplies so you can pack them all properly, leave your home, and hopefully return without a scratch.

How It Can Happen

Nuclear War

Nuclear war can begin in many ways and could be a small exchange between nations or could develop very quickly into an apocalyptic war between all nuclear powers. It could start by a terrorist attack that involves a small yield nuclear device that sparks retaliation from the nation that was attacked.

A nuclear war could also be triggered by accident. In 1983 a nuclear early warning system in Russia malfunctioned and showed that America had launched several intercontinental ballistic missiles. The Russian officer in command quickly realised that the system was incorrect and the report must be false. This happened twice that day and on both occasions, the Russian officer in command put a stop to the alarms. Had he not reacted the Russian system would have launched its missiles against America and would have resulted in a worldwide thermonuclear war. The officer in command who is responsible for averting nuclear war on that day was Stanislav Yevgrafovich Petrov.

During the Cold War and for many years afterwards, there have been many false alarms of enemy attack from scheduled test launches of conventional missiles, which were mistaken for legitimate attacks, to flocks of birds. One such incident occurred when Soviet computers interpreted the sun reflecting off some clouds as the trails from inbound American missiles that had all the hallmarks of nuclear-tipped intercontinental ballistic missiles.

It's not just Russian computer systems that seem to mistake ordinary events as a potential nuclear attack. On two occasions, between 1979 and 1980, **NORAD** (North American Aerospace Defence Command), which is tasked with providing early warning and defence capabilities to Northern America, suffered a significant computer glitch that mistakenly reported a massive Soviet nuclear strike was inbound on mainland United States. No explanation for the glitches was ever given.

If two superpowers are engaged in war or if they are massing troops at their borders in anticipation of war this could lead to one nation inadvertently launching a nuclear weapon if there is any confusion or misinterpretation. Such a scenario will most likely result in a small-scale exchange of

several nukes from each side until things
settle down again.

Economic Collapse

Unless you have been living under a rock
you will be aware of the economic collapse of
2008. Most people on Earth suffered in some
way during this economic disaster while only
a small minority managed to profit from it.
But what if the worldwide economy was to
completely collapse in such a way that all
money became worthless overnight? The
likelihood of such a scenario occurring is very
high.

After World War One Germany faced
massive debts and decided to print more
money in order to pay it all off. This surge in
issuing more money resulted in massive
inflation that increased on a daily basis. As
a result of this, the price of goods and
services rose to unbelievably high levels.
Within only 1 year the inflation rate had
climbed so high that people had to take
wheelbarrows full of cash with them to buy a
loaf of bread, which had soared to record
prices of 201 billion Marks in November
1923. Children were playing with large piles
of discarded cash in the streets while

households burned bundles of cash to keep warm. Imagine if you lived at that time and your life savings were 5,000 Marks, for example. Within a week that money wouldn't buy you anything. To overcome this, people began bartering for goods instead of using the now worthless money.

In order to survive an economic collapse, it is important to have a stock of precious metals, such as Gold and Silver, to use for bartering. If you live in a city it is best advised to leave as soon as possible as instances of looting and violence will become commonplace. You should cultivate a diverse range of resources such as growing your own food that can be traded for the things you need. Some tradable items include:

- Food
- Water
- Seeds
- Animals (chickens, cows, goats, pigs)
- Firewood
- Petroleum and other fuels
- Gold / Silver
- Clothing
- Medicine

Another tradeable item that will be highly sought after is toilet paper because it will become impossible for people to purchase such a luxury, yet necessary, commodity. If you have toilet paper in very large quantities you could potentially trade individual rolls for substantial amounts of goods or services.

One item that should **never** be traded is weapons as these can be used against you and you could lose everything you have worked so hard to gather.

Super Volcano

There are currently 6 supervolcanoes on Earth with each one possessing enough power to cause widespread devastation and death. It would be highly unlikely that more than one of these supervolcanoes would erupt at the same time. The most likely of these to erupt anytime soon is the Yellowstone Caldera in Wyoming USA. This supervolcano erupts every 600,000 years with the most recent eruption occurring 640,000 years ago making the Yellowstone Caldera overdue for an eruption.

The eruption of any super volcano would be as devastating as a worldwide thermonuclear war. If the super volcano in the Yellowstone Caldera was to erupt it will cause a gigantic eruption that will last approximately one week, expelling massive amounts of lava very high into the air. The explosive eruption of lava will continue unhindered during the entire week-long eruption. The higher this lava goes the more it will cool down resulting in it falling back to Earth as a gooey hot rock and will be spread over a distance of approximately 65km (40 miles) from the centre of the eruption. Anything hit by this falling rock will ignite due to the extremely high temperatures of this molten rock.

Ash from this eruption will be expelled to far higher altitudes than the molten rock and will eventually settle in the upper atmosphere where it will stay for several years before eventually falling to Earth or dissipating. Just like a nuclear winter, this ash cloud will prevent sunlight from effectively reaching us. As a result, all plant life on Earth will suffer to the extent that crops will not grow properly for several years resulting in mass starvations of animals and humans that will significantly impact the global human population for several years.

Due to the amounts of people who will die as a result of this nuclear winter style event, it may not be possible for the survivors to bury everyone. Expect millions of dead animals and humans to be left unburied. This will result in widespread diseases such as Cholera, Dysentery and Typhoid.

In order to survive a super volcano eruption, you will need to stock up on enough food to last for up to 4 years.

Asteroid Strike

The probability of a huge asteroid hitting Earth is very high. There are approximately 1 million near-Earth objects that have the potential to enter our atmosphere and cause damage. So far NASA have been able to track about 10,000 of these objects and there are often reports in the media of an asteroid fly-by, sometimes with a few days' notice, but most often we only hear about these incidents after they happen.

For an asteroid to destroy all life on Earth it would have to be approximately 96km (60 miles) wide but this would also depend on the composition of the asteroid, speed and angle of the strike. If you hear news reports of such a large asteroid heading our way it is best if you make the most of the limited time you have left as survival, in this instance, is impossible.

It is possible that a massive asteroid strikes Earth yet still gives mankind the opportunity to survive. The damage caused would depend on the size of the asteroid, speed and angle of the strike as well as the composition of the area on Earth that is struck.

If the impact is on land it will throw up huge amounts of dust that will settle in the upper atmosphere causing a nuclear winter effect that could last for years. This will result in massive food shortages within one growing season. Plants, animals and humans will die off in mass starvations. The average temperature on Earth could drop as much as 20^0C (68^0F) for several years before slowly recovering. These winters will result in further deaths.

If the impact occurs on water it will likely throw large quantities of water vapour into the upper atmosphere. This will result in extended periods of rainfall that could potentially last for years and result in widespread flooding.

Regardless of where an asteroid hits it may result in regional or global earthquakes, tsunamis or widespread climate changes.

As there may never be any warning of such a strike and no possible way to predict precisely where a strike could occur it is impossible to suggest a specific region that best supports continued survival. Maintain a supply of food, water and seeds in order to become as self-sufficient as possible.

Chemical / Biological Warfare

While many believe that chemical weapons have not been used in conventional warfare since World War One, they have been used my military forces from Iraq during the Iraq-Iran war in the 1980s. Iraq also used mustard gas and nerve agents against Kurdish nationals in the city of Halabja in Northern Iraq in 1988.

Records show that biological weapons have been used as far back as 1346 when Mongols catapulted dead bodies, which contaminated with plague, over the walls of Kaffa in Crimea.

While the use of chemical weapons is unlikely in a modern war it cannot be ruled out.   When a country is faced with destruction it is capable of doing anything while trying to survive.   Chemical and biological weapons are held by most developed countries and are stored for future use, even though a lot of those countries have signed up to the Chemical Weapons Convention which was adopted by the Conference on Disarmament in Geneva in 1992.

The most likely scenario of a chemical or biological attack would come from a terrorist organisation.   Such an attack may be directed at a single large city or could be in the form of multiple attacks on large cities scattered around a country in order to cause maximum destruction.

Terrorist organisations could get their hands on abandoned chemical or biological weapons as well as create their own.   It is not that difficult to create a chemical weapon or nerve agent.   Such weapons are desirable because 1 gramme of a toxin has the potential to kill up to 10 million people, depending on the toxic agent used and its deployment.

Should your city be hit by a chemical or biological attack it is vital that you leave as fast as possible.   Protective clothing such as biological suits and gas masks can offer limited protection but only for a short period of time. Use any means at your disposal to get away from the area of attack. Do not become complacent; ensure that you get very far from the city, as most chemical or biological agents will be invisible, tasteless and odourless. Other individuals may be a danger to you as they may be infected with a biological toxin that could easily be spread to you.

Global Tsunami

A global tsunami will most likely be tied to a global quake (*see below*) and will result from multiple fault lines, moving at the same time, along ocean floors and even some land-based fault lines that are close enough to the shore. A massive landslide, occurring at the correct place, along a shoreline can trigger a tsunami to hit the coastline of another continent, possibly thousands of kilometres away from the source. The only other way a global tsunami could occur is if there are dramatic and violent changes in the Earths rotational axes or some other force that violently pushes Earth out of its orbit.

While a global tsunami may not encompass the entire planet it would most likely involve tsunami's striking much of the coastal regions on Earth. These tsunamis may be larger than any we have seen so far in recorded history, depending on the cause.

Tsunamis can cause mass destruction and loss of life in a very short period of time, as seen during the Indian Ocean tsunami of 2004 and the Japan tsunami of 2011. Because of these two disasters, there are now far more early warning systems in place, however, these systems only exist in areas that are prone to tsunamis. If you live in an area that is not currently in danger than the chances are you may not receive any form of advanced warning.

The most widely held belief is that you will first notice the ocean dramatically receding from the shoreline, as was witnessed during the Indian Ocean tsunami of 2004 when the Indonesian town of Bande Ache saw the ocean recede and expose the ocean floor. This phenomenon is known as *Draw-Down*. However, this was not the case in Sri Lanka where the ocean did not recede yet a tsunami hit.

If you are close to a shoreline and notice anything unusual about the sea level, such as a very dramatic rise or fall, it may be a sign of an approaching tsunami and you should take immediate action. Run as far inland as possible and seek out the highest elevation that you can. Do not return to your home to collect your bug-out-bag as tsunamis travel extremely fast with currents that are far too strong to overcome.

Tsunamis can last for several hours and will consist of a series of waves that come one after the other. The speed of a tsunami will be deceptive because the first wave will travel far slower than the next wave. The reason for this is because the first wave creates a non-friction layer that allows the second wave to travel unencumbered thus picking up speed.

If you live on a coastline you may consider hiding a cache of supplies on high ground close to your home, however, the best possible option is to minimise your exposure by moving as far inland as possible.

Tsunami waters have been known to extend inland as far as 1km (0.6 miles) with water levels as low as 30cm (1 foot). Do not become complacent as 30cm of fast flowing water can easily knock you off your feet and result in your death due to currents or debris that is trapped in the water. This fast flowing debris can hinder your ability to regain your footing, pin you under the water or strike you with great force.

Planet X

Planet X, also known as Nibiru, is believed to be one of a group of planets far beyond Pluto with a highly elliptical orbit that brings it closest to Earth once every 3,500 years. The planet's existence was theorised by Zecharia Sitchin, who interpreted ancient Babylonian and Sumerian scripts that spoke about the planet, and also by the American astronomer Percival Lowell who believed that distortions in the orbits of Uranus and Neptune could only be explained by, as yet, undiscovered planets.

There is no scientific basis for the existence of Planet X which makes this scenario highly unlikely.

The 3,500-year elliptical orbit of these planets is believed to cause massive disruption on Earth as they approach the Sun on their closest pass towards us. The severity of the disruptions cannot be accurately predicted but would likely cause massive earthquakes, tsunamis, volcanic eruptions, tilting or repositioning of Earth and extreme disruptions to our climate. Such disruptions would likely see crop harvests failing, resulting in large scale global famine. Another potential effect of Planet X's approach could be a pole shift (reversal of Earth's magnetic poles) which will result in the crust being dramatically moved. This movement over a short period of time will cause climate changes that will destroy all planetary systems to such an extent it may result in the extinction of all life on Earth.

Believers in Planet X and its disastrous approach to Earth claim that, as the planet enters our Solar System its gravitational influence will cause meteorites and asteroids in the asteroid belt, beyond Mars, to be flung towards Earth. Should Planet X enter our Solar System expect asteroid strikes that could potentially last for months.

As this event has never occurred before and is unfounded in the scientific community it is impossible to suggest a definitive method of survival, however maintaining a survival mindset and storing sufficient quantities of food and water are essential for surviving any disaster situation.

Evacuating to an underground shelter may also provide a measure of survival due to asteroid strikes and potential disruptions to our atmosphere that may make above-ground survival difficult or impossible. Many ancient underground facilities have been found which may suggest that Earth could have suffered an airborne attack such as; large-scale asteroid strikes or other disruptions that occurred over a long period of time. Perhaps the stories of Planet X are true after all!

Solar Flare / E.M.P.

Solar flares are eruptions of high-energy radiation that originate from the surface of the Sun and have the potential to travel to Earth where they have been known to interfere with electrical and electronic equipment. Should a sizeable enough solar flare hit Earth it could wipe out all electronic and electrical devices. The damage caused would be permanent and the affected device would have to be either scrapped or rebuilt in order for it to function again. An EMP (Electromagnetic Pulse) is usually caused by nuclear weapons and has the same effect on electronic devices as a solar flare.

Should a devastating solar flare of global proportions strike Earth it will cause mass blackouts across entire countries as well as widespread destruction of electronic devices. If you are trapped in an elevator you will need to figure out how to escape on your own as the chances of rescue are now remote. Remember that all electronic devices will fail, including the computers in vehicles so the fire service or paramedics will not be able to reach you.

Electrical transformers, as well as full substations and power plants, will also fail. Every electronic device in these systems will need to be rebuilt from scratch and reinstalled in order to get electrical power to flow again, however, the factories where these devices are made will also be out of commission. Creating new electronic devices in factories that are no longer capable of making them will result in an extremely slow recovery.

The only way to protect any electronic devices is to use a Faraday Cage, which is a metal box that is earthed and contains a shelf to house your electronic devices in such a way as they cannot touch the interior of the box. Such devices will prevent electromagnetic interference by redirecting energy through the box and into the ground. Items on the shelf inside the Faraday Cage remain unaffected.

If you live in a city during this event it is best if you leave your home and exit the city as soon as possible. It will not be possible to start vehicles so don't waste your time on these and be prepared to walk out of the city. The chances of electrical power being re-established in any meaningful way, during your lifetime, are highly unlikely.

Global Quake

A global quake is highly unlikely but not beyond the bounds of possibility. Should the Earth's core experience dramatic changes, or the Solar System drift into a region of space where gravitational forces become so strong as to cause dramatic changes to the core, then the Earth may experience a global quake or a series of earthquakes that occur one after the other.

If you live in an earthquake-prone region of Earth or you live near a fault line, whether it is active or not, you are already in a danger zone and must take the necessary action to move to a safe area. If a global quake occurs it may create new fault lines in areas that were once clear.

Regardless of where you are when a global quake strikes you will most likely feel significant tremors. It is a possibility that any early warning systems in place may fail due to the severity of the quake and the widespread destruction caused. You may not receive any warnings as a result.

Animals have been known to give an indication of a coming earthquake, however, these warning signs will only manifest seconds before the actual quake. Some domestic animals such as dogs or cats have been known to suddenly jump up and run in blind panic seconds before a major quake. In January 2010 a guide dog named Sophie was with its owner in an office block in North Carolina. Seconds before a 6.5 magnitude earthquake hit, CCTV captures the dog getting up and running for cover. Ancient

Greek writings describe how in c. 353 BC., animals such as rats and snakes deserted the city of Helice days before an earthquake struck. It is believed that animals can sense slight instabilities in the crust of the Earth that could warn of an impending earthquake. You will not be able to accurately rely on the behaviour of animals to predict a quake as these warnings may come only seconds before the actual earthquake strikes.

Should a global earthquake strike it is important to note that you will not receive any help or assistance from any governmental organisation. This is because such a disaster is far too big for them to cope with. It is up to you to survive.

When you feel an earthquake it is vital that you leave any building you are in immediately and seek out any form of open land. If you are in a city you should try to get to a park, the outskirts of town or any other open area. Ensure that you are not near any trees, electrical pylons or other tall objects that can be toppled over and crush you. If going outside is not possible you should seek shelter under a sturdy table or stand in the frame of a doorway. It would be unwise to seek shelter in a basement as these areas could become covered in falling debris and you may find yourself trapped.

As soon as the initial quake is over you should get out of any building you are in. If possible, grab your bug-out-bag as you leave. Many aftershocks will follow the initial quake and could be just as powerful as the first one. If your house seems to be structurally unsound it is best if you abandon it immediately and leave the city. Do not attempt to re-enter your home to fetch supplies. It is important to leave the city as widespread looting and violence will follow the initial quake resulting in your city becoming a dangerous environment.

Fire will become a big problem following the initial quake as gas mains rupture. Do not expect the fire service to be in a position to tackle all the blazes as they will be redeployed by the government to facilitate their needs. If you smell gas while evacuating from the city it is best if you avoid that area, even if this means taking a long detour, as that gas cloud could erupt in flames at any moment.

Pandemic

A pandemic is an epidemic of some form of infectious disease that spreads rapidly throughout the human population, often over large areas of Earth or even worldwide. This scenario is very probably and should be carefully considered when prepping.

During World War One it was not unusual for soldiers to die from influenza. Dozens of soldiers from either side used to die from the flu every year until a new flu virus began to spread through the trenches in 1918. Soldiers often lived in very close quarters with pigs and other animals that were being used as food to feed armies. In some cases, soldiers were dying within 24 hours of showing symptoms of this new flu virus. This new type of flu went unreported in most areas except in Spain resulting in the name *Spanish Flu*.

It is believed that this new strain of flu began in pigs, mutated and spread among soldiers. Unfortunately, the timing couldn't have been worse, as the war had just ended and all soldiers were returning home. People began getting sick in all areas of the world and it is believed that up to 500 million people were infected worldwide. Considering that the population of Earth was 1.8 billion in 1918, this represents around 27% of all people becoming infected. In today's figures, this would translate to approximately 1.9 billion people becoming infected. The amount of deaths attributed to Spanish Flu is between 50 and 100 million people.

This flu initially mutated in pigs just like its modern day equivalent H1N1 (swine flu). The unusual thing about these flu epidemics is that they tend to kill relatively young healthy people while the elderly and very young tend to survive. This is because the immune system is usually responsible for ultimately killing victims. As the immune system of young healthy people tends to be stronger it will fight harder and exacerbate the symptoms that result in death.

Should a pandemic strike your country, city or town it is vital that you confine yourself and minimise your exposure to other people. Having biohazard suits and gas masks may not be enough to stay safe but are certainly better than not having them. While the pandemic continues ensure that your personal hygiene is maintained and that you thoroughly wash your hands after handling any people or animals.

Global Famine

Global famine is a scenario that is very likely to occur. In the last 100 years, over 35 million people have died as a direct result of food shortages brought about by famine. There are currently 19 countries suffering alarming food shortages or full famines. At the time of writing, there are 805 million people who struggle with hunger on a daily basis and 1.2 billion people who live in extreme poverty. Over 3 billion people live on less than USD$2.50 per day.

A global famine can come about by a number of factors coming together to create extreme food shortages. Transport infrastructure, from trucks to cargo ships, are required for the effective delivery of food to your local store. What if all transport failed overnight? Did you know that your local store or supermarket only has 3 days' supply of food? The only thing that keeps the shelves stocked is our modern transport system.

If Earth was hit by a devastating EMP (Electromagnetic Pulse), drought and an infestation of crop-destroying parasites, at the same time than people around the world will suffer extreme starvation within 1 or 2 weeks. After the first 3 days, all food stocks will have been emptied. While emergency stocks are stored by governments and the military to cover such scenarios, do not expect to be issued with any food as there will be far too many people to feed.

All it would take is for 1 years' worth of crops to fail in all regions of the world to cause extreme problems. Should a global famine be caused by drought that persists for more than 6 months it is vital that you abandon your home and travel to a cooler climate in order to find water and arable land for growing your own food. A global drought could be caused by and extreme change in global climates or a shift in Earth's orbit that brings it dramatically and quickly into an orbit that is closer to the Sun.

In order to prepare in advance, dedicate an area of your garden for growing your own food. Once the shelves in stores have been picked clean, this small amount of self-grown food may be the difference between life and death.

Alien Invasion

The chances of an alien race invading Earth is highly unlikely but not beyond the bounds of possibility. In our galaxy, the Milky Way, it is estimated that over 40 billion Earth-sized planets are orbiting within the habitable zones of their stars. The chances of one or more of those planets containing an advanced, space-faring, civilisation is high. One of those civilisations could be headed our way right now.

There could be many varying reasons for aliens to attack us, such as; to colonise our planet, for our natural resources, or simply because they deem us to be a possible future threat.

The first step before an attack would most likely be a series of reconnaissance missions by the aliens in order to identify strategic targets of importance that they would take out during the initial attack. If the alien race is technologically advanced enough to reach us, these early missions would most likely be done using unmanned craft or some form of robotic soldiers in order to minimise the aliens' exposure to danger.

Should aliens attack they will most likely spend some time in positioning their military forces around our planet in order to strike targets simultaneously. The types or weapons that they could use and their destructive power is impossible to predict but would probably have an equivalent destructive power of our nuclear weapons. Such weapons may or may not leave radioactive fallout.

Following the initial attack, it would be assumed that a ground assault would follow. Depending on the size of the alien force this could range in the millions of soldiers that will most likely be accompanied by advanced drones and robotic type soldiers.

The weaponry that they employ will probably be inconceivable to us, but like all weapons, they will be designed to kill as efficiently as possible. Aliens would probably be able to detect humans even if they are in hiding, just like infrared cameras on police helicopters today.

The best chance of survival would be to hide as far underground as possible. Large stocks of food and water will be necessary as going back outside could become far too dangerous.

Laws and the Military

Before any of these disasters unfold it is vital that you live within the laws that govern your country. If you commit a crime you may find yourself incarcerated in a prison which, depending on the particular disaster, could easily result in your death as the prison could be abandoned by the authorities. Do not get in trouble with the law. Ensure you pay your taxes, drive within the speed limit and do not draw any unwanted attention to yourself. If you are currently serving probation it is even more important for you to not only obey the law but also distance yourself from any individuals that are not law abiding citizens, as hanging around with these people could land you in trouble again.

Nuclear War

Depending on the country you live in and the initial destruction caused to the infrastructure due to nuclear strikes, your governmental structure may collapse shortly after the beginning of the war. Most countries around the world have emergency plans in place for such an event. If central government should fail, power will be transferred to a system of local official's dispersed across the country that will be responsible for small regions. Most governments already have plans in place to allow these regional political systems to take full control of the area they are responsible for and enact any laws they deem as necessary for the continued survival of that region. It will ultimately take many years for the government to regain some semblance of their previous power or it might never happen in your lifetime.

Military forces will be deployed within a day of the initial attacks and will begin taking control of any food or fuel sources that they find. Should there be a warning, such as; a small-scale nuclear exchange between armies, all known subversives in your country will be arrested before the nuclear war begins.

If you are living in America you may find that the military are rounding people up to take them to a safe, secure facility (FEMA camp). **Do not go with them**. FEMA camps are not reliable during or after a nuclear war. It took FEMA 5 days to get water to the Superdome following hurricane Katrina that struck New Orleans in 2005. FEMA camps are specifically designed to keep you contained within the fences. You do not want to be in one of these camps during or after a nuclear war.

Small regional authorities will enact sweeping changes to laws that govern criminal activity such as looting. Military and police forces will be given the authority to shoot looters or any other criminal who tries to flee. Looters or other criminals who are shot while attempting to flee will be stripped of their clothing and any supplies they have. Their bodies will be left where they are as there is no manpower available for the disposal of bodies.

Those who get arrested will be brought to detention camps. As these camps will begin to fill up quickly, special courts will be set up to deal with these growing numbers of criminals. Most crimes will only have one punishment, the death penalty. Police and soldiers will be tasked with not only preventing crime but also with carrying out executions. All conventional laws and courts will be suspended in favour of military tribunal. Do not expect any sympathy being granted to you if you are brought before one of these tribunals. There will be no version of death row and those sentenced to death will be killed within minutes or hours of their sentence being handed down.

Economic Collapse

During a devastating economic collapse, which will be far worse than even the Great Depression of the 1930's, there will be mass forced repossession of property. The repossessions could easily extend beyond property that is in mortgage arrears. Expect all of your possessions to be at risk. Laws will be passed to ensure that all processions and property can easily be reprocessed.

Food rationing will be rigorously enforced which may extend to forced labour in exchange for food. Expect cash to become worthless during this time.

As the situation gets worse and people begin to riot and loot supplies expect curfews to be enacted and enforced. There may be a period of time in which Martial Law is enforced in order to keep control of the population.

As the planet's governments are currently converging into a singular world government it would be expected that the economic collapse would affect most, if not every, country in the World.

If you are caught looting, do not expect any sympathy as you will most likely be shot on sight. New courts will be set up to deal with debt defaulters, which will constitute a significant proportion of the population. Expect debt defaulters, who are found guilty, to be initially fined heavily, later this will extend to prison sentences as the situation gets worse. Many people will be forced into free labour schemes where they will receive far less than minimum wage. These forced labour schemes will be similar to internships, popular with university graduates in America.

After a number of years expect your government to accept a new currency that will most likely see money return to the old system of being backed by Gold. Once this new currency comes into effect it will still take many years for a full recovery.

Super Volcano

Should there be any kind of advanced warning, expect forced mandatory evacuations within a 40km (25 miles) range of the affected area, let's take Yellowstone as an example. Expect mass troop movements across America as well as all U.S. troops returning home from foreign deployment.

Either before or during the actual eruption a state of Marshal Law will be enacted across the entire United States in order to better control the population. Those who are evacuated from the affected area will most likely be housed in FEMA camps.

Within 24 hours after the initial eruption expect emergency procedures to be implemented in North and South America, as well as Asia and parts of Western Europe.

International aid will not be sent to America because all other countries will wait to see exactly what will happen. As the situation gets worse, with nuclear winter now imminent across the globe, all food stores will be put on lockdown and guarded by the military. Food rationing will begin within 2 to 4 weeks after the initial eruption.

A state of Martial Law will most likely be enacted in all other developed countries within 2 weeks of the initial eruption in order to keep control.

As with most other global disasters, expect sweeping changes to the law that will allow soldiers and police forces to shoot looters on sight. Special military tribunals may be set up in various countries to deal with the mass breaches of these new laws. In countries that do not currently have the death penalty, expect that this will be re-instated.

Depending on what country you are in you may be rounded up and forced into working on food production.

The American economy will most likely collapse, which in turn will most likely bring about the collapse of several other countries' economies including; United Kingdom, all EU member states, China and Russia. If this economic collapse occurs expect the same sanctions as described in "*Economic Collapse*" above.

Asteroid Strike

This scenario is a little difficult to carefully scrutinise as it would depend on the size, composition and speed of the asteroid as well as the impact sight. Let's say the asteroid is 20km (12.5 miles) wide and comprises 25% nickel, 15% iron, 50% rock and 10% ice. This would not be the heaviest; most dense object so would not cause a global extinction but would cause massive amounts of damage to Earth, our infrastructure and climate. Let's also assume that the asteroid will strike approximately 400km (249 miles) off the Western coast of France, between the Southern tip of Ireland and the Northern tip of Spain.

Even though this asteroid will be striking the Atlantic Ocean it will still be hitting bedrock and will cause a crater 1.5km (1 mile) deep and 375km (233 miles) wide. Expect an initial earthquake of magnitude 11 at the moment of impact. Most of Europe, Americas East coast and South Americas East coast will be wiped out in the tsunamis that follow the impact.

As this event will devastate much of the globe during impact and in the coming years, expect full Martial Law to be enacted in all countries. Forced mandatory evacuations of, in some cases, entire countries, may be ordered. Food production will drop dramatically in these coming years resulting in food rationing as well as forced labour in exchange for food.

This event has the potential for being an apocalyptic strike against mankind and as a result, it is impossible to correctly gauge what other laws may or may not be implemented during this time. It may be possible that all laws go out the window and we return to a system of *survival of the fittest*. If this is the case then you will need to learn how to effectively kill in order to survive.

Chemical / Biological Warfare

During a chemical or biological attack it is highly likely, depending on the severity of the attack, that your government will implement martial law in order to keep internal control and allow the authorities to take actions they may not have been previously allowed to, such as; stop and search, property seizure, mandatory evacuations or to enforce curfews.

Should the chemical or biological attack be country-wide it is highly likely that all known subversives in your country will be arrested in order for the government to maintain control and quell all possible dissidence. These arrests would happen within the first few days.

If you are living in a large town or city that is directly attacked or close to an area directly affected by an attack you may face mandatory evacuations. If the military or police begin rounding people up it is best to go with them as standing your ground may result in your arrest. Should the attacks be country-wide, to such an extent as it is causing the full collapse of your country, there may be summary executions carried out by military or police forces. These actions are against the Geneva Convention on Human Rights and while there is no legal loophole that allows for such executions they may still happen.

Depending on the severity of the attack there may be a state of emergency or martial law that extends from 1 month up to several years. Should the attack be attributed to a sovereign nation expect your country to immediately go to war. If this is the case it is possible that a conscription law is enacted forcing individuals to serve in the military for a fixed term, usually 1 year.

Global Tsunami

The most likely scenario concerning changes in laws following a global tsunami is that all laws should remain unchanged. Depending on the severity of damage caused to your country there may be temporary states of emergency enacted in order to allow the military to take over from the police force for the purposes of maintaining order.

The only other possible outcome is that new laws are created to force citizens to help in any relief effort, clean-up, or body disposal. These changes in law will only be temporary and will probably only last for several months, at the most.

As this will be a global event it is unlikely that international aid will ever be deployed either to or from your country. Each nation will be far too busy and their resources far too stretched to be in a position to help you.

Planet X

If Planet X exists and if it enters our Solar System and causes the widespread damaged outlined in the above chapter "*How It Can Happen*" then expect all laws and systems of government to systematically fail throughout the planet. Whole countries will fall into a state of widespread chaos. In such lawless circumstances, there will be no one in a position to help you or protect you. It is important that you remain alert to danger and be prepared to kill if necessary.

The only law that could possibly exist in this scenario is the law of the jungle. Governments, both regional and national, will become a thing of the past. There will no longer be court systems or prisons. It will be likely that people will live in small groups and will protect their territory and companions by any means necessary. It will become extremely dangerous to attempt to contact or trade with these groups.

Solar Flare / E.M.P.

During the initial phases of the electrical blackouts expect widespread looting. While police forces are dealing with looters there will also be emergency services trying to help people who are trapped and in need of assistance. As time goes on expect laws to be enacted that deal very harshly with looters.

Depending on the level of lawlessness that will follow it may become necessary for governments to enact Martial Law in order to keep control of the population.

Because our modern day society heavily relies on electronic transfer of funds, the resulting global blackout may see the collapse of economies around the world within the first few days. Should this be the case expect laws to be enacted in the same way as described in the section *"Economic Collapse"* above.

All international trade will stop on the first day of the global blackout. Expect all trade ships and oil tankers to be turned around and return to their port of origin. You may be forced to work in return for food.

Global Quake

During and after a global quake, the devastation will be so severe and widespread that police and military forces will most likely be operating on their own terms, especially within the first week. This will be due to the widespread devastation caused to communication infrastructure and panic on their part.

During this first week, expect the military and police forces to be performing summary executions on criminals and imposing curfews or mass evacuations. These curfews and mass evacuations can be spread to various random zones around an urban area, so you may be under a curfew while your friend or family member on the other side of the city may be evacuated to a new area where no such curfew exists.

Looting will be widespread and deadly. Expect the risk of death from, not only police and military but also from fellow looters. People will be extremely desperate for survival and will do anything it takes in order to survive.

Once things settle down a bit and communication is re-established there is a chance that governments will impose strict curfews for all citizens that could last for months or up to one year. Forced labour in exchange for food will probably be enforced within the first month and last for anywhere up to 5 years. This forced labour will most likely be used for food production, the clearing of rubble, and the disposal of the dead.

While economies will most likely survive there will be a period of time where all trade, worldwide, will be suspended. Expect massive inflation with a possible stabilisation occurring after approximately 10 years. You may be prevented from purchasing certain properties or even your rights to own your home may be suspended and all properties handed to the control of the state.

Pandemic

Should a devastating pandemic strike the globe it will most likely result in curfews being imposed along with laws to prevent people gathering in groups. This will be the first stage in a long list of widespread changes to laws that will slowly occur, over time, as the situation gets worse. Laws will be enacted to force whole communities or towns into quarantine with the military protecting these areas. Expect the military to shoot on sight, anyone who attempts to escape from these protected zones.

Should a country have such a large level of exposure to a deadly pathogen than expect the international community to impose a full quarantine on that country with nobody allowed to enter or leave. International military forces may be deployed to guard the coastline of such a country with a view to destroying any ships or aeroplanes that try to leave.

It may not be possible, or permitted, for people to shop in their local store so food will be distributed by the military and police forces.

Mandatory vaccinations will be enforced once a drug is found to combat either the pathogen or its symptoms. It is also possible that forced evacuations are carried out in some areas.

Should the situation get to levels that are deemed out of control, it is possible that laws will be enacted to move the sick and dying to concentration camps in order to protect the healthy. Population culling may become a part of internment in the concentration camps, similar to what happened to political decedents, the elderly and infirm, during World War Two under the NAZI regime.

If you display symptoms of the pathogen during this time you are at risk, not only from military and police forces but also from other people who would be terrified of contracting the disease.

It is best if you stay at home as much as possible and away from exposure to people, as you may or may not know who is sick and who is not.

Global Famine

If a global famine was to hit in a single growing season the first thing you will notice is a massive increase in inflation and the prices of food. The ability to purchase even the most basic food supplies would fall out of the range of most people on Earth. Riots and looting would quickly follow as people would become desperate after 3 days without food.

Expect the police to be given new powers to deal harshly with looters. Food stocks would become heavily guarded and food distribution would begin within the first month. Expect severe food rationing during the first year of a global famine.

Rights to land ownership would most likely be suspended as vast stretches of land will be repossessed by governments and zoned for food production only. Any seed banks or stores that sell seeds will have their stocks confiscated by the government and put towards regional food production schemes.

Laws may be enacted in order to force civilians to attempt food production in their gardens. There may be a new law that would see civilians serve a mandatory term to be used as farmhands or in other areas of mass food production. This will be similar to national service which sees certain civilians being forced to serve a term of, usually 1 year, in military service.

The death rate during this event may be on a scale not seen before. As a result, there may be a mandatory term for the survivors that will see them removing and disposing of bodies. Do not expect a dignified burial during this time as any bodies recovered will be either buried in mass graves or incinerated.

Alien Invasion

During the initial phases of an alien invasion, governments may change some laws or create new ones that will limit the amount of food people can purchase in a given day. Expect soldiers and police forces to call upon the homes of any gun owners to confiscate their ammunition or maybe their weapons as well. This confiscated ammunition and weapons will be distributed to military and police forces around the world in preparation for an attack.

Curfews may be enforced and areas of strategic importance will be evacuated. New laws that allow military forces to place missile batteries on top of civilian buildings will also be enacted.

As the alien spacecraft begin to position themselves around the planet expect mandatory military conscription on a mass level. All able-bodied individuals will be literally round up on the street and brought to a military base for basic training, which will be no more than 24-hours, unless the attack has already begun, in which case you will be brought straight to the front lines.

During World War Two, Soviet Russia used military trucks to round-up people and bring them to Stalingrad, where the German forces had already taken half of the city. These young men were brought straight to the front lines, without any form of training. Because supplies were very limited they were put in pairs with one soldier carrying a rifle containing 5 rounds of ammunition and the other soldier was given a magazine containing 5 rounds of ammunition. Should the soldier with the rifle fall in battle, the second soldier would pick up the rifle and continue fighting.

These young men had no training of any kind and were sent straight into battle; expect the same during an alien invasion.

After the initial attack and the beginning of the ground invasion expect all laws to become unenforceable with governments collapsing and military forces being scattered and disorganised.

Avoiding the military

Avoiding the military or police forces would be necessary during the following emergencies;

- Nuclear War
- Super Volcano
- Asteroid Strike
- Chemical / Biological Warfare
- Planet X

- Pandemic

During these types of scenarios, the military and police forces will become dangerous and will not be able to help you.

Like most preppers around the world, you are probably stockpiling supplies in order to survive, however, if you use a credit card or even a store loyalty card the government know you are stockpiling and will gather any information they need to in order to find out where your supplies are kept. Algorithms are in use in most large stores around the globe that can keep track of what people are buying. These algorithms will flag anything out of the ordinary, so if you buy 200 tubes of toothpaste your government will want to know why. Always pay for stockpile items with cash only.

A far better system is if you can form a trade agreement with the store owner. Maybe you grow your own food. A basket of fresh fruit and vegetables, that you would ordinarily throw out because it is surplus, can get you some supplies.

There are TV shows about preppers and prepping where individuals show their supplies and plans. These people have exposed themselves to not only the military but to people in their neighbourhood who will now know that they have food and other survival supplies. In the event of a real emergency, these people will become targets. The military wants your supplies and will simply drive up to your front door and take anything they want during an emergency.

Be a smart prepper; do not let anyone know that you are stockpiling supplies or where you are hiding them. Do not risk your supplies being confiscated, they are your supplies and should be protected.

If you live in a city during one of the above disasters you will need to leave immediately. If your family are trying to encourage you to stay you must force them out of the city or make the difficult choice to leave them behind if they will not follow you. Do not wait around to see if you will be rescued because there will be nothing that the military or police can do for you during one of these emergencies. Once you leave the city, do not expect to return ever again. If you have left something at home, even something vital to survival, it is best if you continue your escape as returning home could be fatal. Everything can change within seconds during such emergencies.

The best place to go during one of the above emergencies is an isolated house deep in the countryside. If it is difficult for you to get there it will be difficult for others to get there also. Keep this in mind when selecting a new home.

Looting

Expect widespread looting to occur during or shortly after the following disasters;

- Nuclear War
- Economic Collapse
- Super Volcano
- Asteroid Strike
- Solar Flare / EMP
- Global Quake
- Global Famine

Within the first 3 days of a disastrous event, all products will be stripped from shelves. Expect vital supplies such as food and water to be gone within the first day or two. Shops only store about 3 days' worth of food as they rely on constant deliveries in order to replenish their supply. The above events will render such deliveries impossible very quickly.

Looting supplies will be extremely dangerous and should be avoided if possible. Should your prepping supplies be lost, or you didn't gather any supplies, you should loot for supplies as soon as possible, but be advised that this can be far too dangerous and you may not survive. Military and police forces will probably be deployed to urban areas in order to prevent looting and they will most likely shoot on sight. It doesn't matter if the supplies you've taken are life-saving items such as food or water, if you are approached by a police officer or soldier you must drop your looted supplies and run away as fast as you can. Get under cover when you can and make your way home.

Depending on the particular disaster scenario it will be impossible to plead your case with police or military personnel while looting. They will be trigger-happy, under orders to shoot, scared and probably suffering from their own hardships and will shoot you. Try looting another day or in another location if you need to.

Currency and Trade

The following disasters will most likely not affect the global financial system to such an extent that economies suffer from rapid inflation or dramatic fluctuations that would require you to store tradable commodities. If you are prepping for any of the following it may be a waste of time and effort to horde Gold or Silver bullion. Your funds would be better used in purchasing tangible items such as food and water.

- Chemical / Biological Warfare
- Global Tsunami
- Global Quake
- Pandemic
- Global Famine

The following disaster scenarios will not wipe out the financial system as we know it but will most likely result in inflation and increased prices of vital commodities such as food and water. In planning for these events it is prudent to gather a supply of Gold and

Silver bullion as well as tradable items such as food, fresh water, firewood etc.

- Super Volcano
- Economic Collapse
- Asteroid Strike

With the final four scenarios all currencies and financial systems as you know them will fail miserably. Even Gold and Silver bullion will become useless as nobody will have a use for these metals. The only tradable commodities will be food, fresh water, protective clothing and even shelter. Do not expect financial systems or currencies to return within your lifetime.

- Nuclear War
- Planet X
- Alien Invasion

If you receive any form of warning of an impending global disaster that you know is guaranteed to wipe out the financial system it may be possible within the first few days to withdraw all of your cash from the bank and use these funds to purchase emergency supplies, water or food. Credit cards may also be used during these first few days but be aware that you could find yourself in considerable debt if the disaster does not unfold or if the financial systems remain intact. You may also be able to trade any household valuables or decorative items for water or food.

In most disaster cases the most valuable commodity you could have is fresh, clean, uncontaminated water. Everybody needs water to survive and a person cannot go for more than a few days without it. Having a well or access to a stream plus the necessary filtering and decontamination equipment could prove to be very valuable and must be hidden and protected at all costs.

During most types of disasters, people will become desperate and trigger happy. For this reason, it is vital that if you decide to approach others for the purposes of making a trade, or if they approach you for the same reason, you must not let them know where you live or what you have stored. People will be more than willing to kill in order to steal your supplies or gain access to your shelter.

During any trade situation always remain on full alert and do not put yourself into a position where the other people could confine you, render you unconscious or otherwise gain the upper hand against you. Do not accept any gifts such as a drink or food as these could be spiked with drugs. The first trade with anyone will be a dangerous but sometimes necessary endeavour.

Should you establish a regular trade with any individual or group do not become complacent and always remain in a defensive high-alert mode as you will not be able to trust others. It may be possible to slowly build up a level of trust that could result in regularly working together with others or even grouping together permanently.

Bug-Out Bag

During any disaster situation, it is vital that you can leave your current area, if necessary, at a moment's notice. This is known as bugging-out and is practised by, not only prepper's but also military personnel. What if disaster struck right now, while you are reading this book? What would you grab and take with you if you had to leave your home and you only had 2 minutes to prepare? You might take a bottle of water, some paperwork like your driver's license, your keys, some sentimental items, wallet and a sharp kitchen knife. How can you possibly survive for any length of time on these supplies? What if your car won't start because of an event like a solar flare or E.M.P? Maybe you live in a large city and don't own a car because you always took public transport, but what if the public transport network has also failed? You now need to walk out of your city with very little to no supplies during a major catastrophic event. Will the clothes you are wearing right now be sufficient to survive cold nights when you don't have any shelter?

You may need to keep on the move for the rest of your life but you won't survive for very long unless you have the necessary supplies to survive for the first 3 days. Most prepper's, military, survivalists and even the CDC (Centers for Disease Control and Prevention) advocate having enough supplies to survive, without assistance, for at least 3 days.

Your bug-out bag should contain those 3 days' worth of vital supplies. This will be the one thing you grab when you need to leave your city or town with only a moment's notice. It should contain every possible item to ensure, not only survival but also shelter and tools to help you gather food and water after those 3 days are up.

Keep your bug-out bag close to you at all times. Some preppers will leave this bag by their front door and drive to work in the morning. But what if disaster struck while they were at work? Their essential supplies are now at home and they may not be able to travel home to retrieve them or the journey home could take so much time that they remain trapped in a dangerous city.

During the Vietnam War, U.S. soldiers adopted a policy of always keeping their rifle within arm's reach, no matter where they were or what they were doing. Those soldiers who did not adopt this policy were usually killed quickly in a firefight. Adopt this same principle and keep your bug-out bag within reach. Always bring your bug-out bag in the trunk of your car when driving anywhere.

One of the main principles when gathering supplies for a bug-out bag is to only pack the essential supplies needed to survive for 3 days. Do not pack unnecessary items or sentimental items as these only take up space that could be used for something that could mean the difference between life and death. It is perfectly okay to leave sentimental items behind.

Supplies

You should gather all the supplies for your bug-out bag **before** considering the bag itself. Too many preppers' have made the mistake of purchasing the backpack first, only to discover that all the supplies will not fit. I will talk more about the backpack a little later in this chapter.

- Wrist watch

This should be a wind-up watch. You can either wind this watch every day (preferred option) or you can check the time before bugging out and set the watch then.

- Compass
- Large torch
- Small torch
- Headlamp
- Wind-up torch
- Batteries x10
- Anglers' glow sticks

When it comes to things like torches or ignition sources it is important to bring multiple types because if you only bring one item it may fail, or it may be exposed to environmental conditions that render it useless, such as water damage, etc. Don't rely on a single type of battery; take different make and models with you. Rechargeable batteries can also be useful if you also pack a solar charger.

Anglers' glow sticks are very small and are designed to be attached to a fishing line, as a float, for night time fishing. These small glow lights will provide enough light to illuminate your tent, for example, and usually produce light for up to 10 hours. Bring as many of these glow sticks as you can carry.

- Drinking water x6 litres (12.7 pints)
- Water purification tablets x10
- Water filter
- Collapsible water bottle (20 litres (42.3 pints) capacity)
- Condoms x4

The human body can only survive for approximately 3 days without water after which time you **will** die. By bringing a filter and purification tablets you ensure that any water source you come across on your travels can be filtered before drinking. It is highly advised to also boil any water you find to ensure that all pathogens have been killed.

In the case of Nuclear War, Chemical / Biological Warfare, Pandemic and Alien Invasion, it may not be possible to successfully clean water of radioactive sources or diseases. Under such circumstances, it will be risky to consume unknown sources of water.

You can hold up to 2 litres (4.2 pints) of water in a condom when needed.

- Tinned food x5
- MREs (Meals Ready to Eat) x5
- Small fishing kit
- Snare wire
- Can opener (P-38)
- Camping stove
- Cooking pot
- Eating utensils

Bring enough food to last for 3 days as well as basic hunting equipment so you can trap new sources of food. Have as much variety of food as possible. Attempt to bring foods that can simulate a normal day, one type for breakfast, another type for dinner, etc.

The camping stove that you choose should be one that you add your own kindling too. Gas cooking stoves only add extra weight with the gas canister. This is weight that you don't need to be carrying and leaves you extra space for other essential supplies.

- Local ordinance survey map
- Compact survival guide
- Compact first aid book

There will never be a need to bring any complex maps of the World or even your own country. During a real emergency, you will not be able to move very far. The best map is a detailed ordinance survey map of your local region or of the region you intend to escape to.

These items should be sealed in zip-lock bags and/or shrink wrap to ensure that they do not get destroyed by water damage.

- Survival knife
- Multi-tool
- Entrenching tool
- Small axe
- Machete

There is no need to carry complex tools, just learn how to survive with basic equipment. You only have a limited amount of space in order to pack all of your supplies and remember, you will have to carry all of it. An entrenching tool is vital for building a latrine (makeshift toilet) when you settle down for the night.

- Butane lighters x5
- Matches x5 packs
- Permanent match lighter
- Flint lighter
- Lighter fluid x2
- Magnifying glass

During an emergency, the ability to build and light a fire can mean the difference between life and death. Just like your batteries, do not rely on one single source. What if you only brought matches and they got wet? Permanent match lighters use lighter fluid as their fuel source and a single filling can last for up to 15,000 match strikes.

Flint lighters only produce a spark and the magnifying glass is reliant on the sun so these will become a last resort option.

- First Aid kit
- Scissors
- Medical gauze
- Extra bandages

First aid supplies, while they hopefully will never be needed, are absolutely vital for any emergency situation. The standard first aid kits that you can purchase from your local store are pretty much worthless. Get a first aid kit from a dedicated survival store or prepper supply website. The scissors you select should be capable of cutting through thick leather boots. Should you ever run out of bandages you can create some from T-shirts. Be sure to boil these to kill any germs or other nasty things that may be on the clothing.

- Journal
- Several pens and pencils
- Non-fragrant soap
- Deck of playing cards
- Small towel
- Travel size toothbrush
- Toothpaste

During any emergency situation, it is vital to keep your spirits up. This, in turn, will keep your survivalist mindset active and this boost in your general mood can keep you going during bad times.

Personal hygiene plays a major role in boosting your mood and should be undertaken every day. When you are clean it is one thing you don't need to worry about during an emergency. Keeping your mind as active as possible is another vital boosting activity. When some free time is available read a book or play a game with your deck of cards.

Write in your journal daily, about any possible food or water sources you come across and also about your current mood.

Keep track of the days by ticking them off the calendar inside of the journal.

Gratitude is one of the biggest things for keeping your spirits high. If you think in terms of being grateful for the things you have and not think about the things you have lost through the emergency situation then you will not only boost your general mood but you will also increase your chances of long-term survival by increasing your survivalist mindset.

- Tent
- Sleeping bag
- Warm blanket
- Large tarp
- Ground mat

Shelter is very important for surviving during an emergency. We are used to living in warm houses with all the modern conveniences they provide, but when you are on the move you must rely on the basics. If the emergency you face is; Nuclear War, Super Volcano, Asteroid Strike or Planet X, expect temperatures to drop dramatically within the first 24-hours from the start of the event. Average global temperatures could be very low for many years.

The tent you choose should be capable of keeping the wind and rain out as well as providing enough space for housing you and all of your supplies. You may be living in this tent for a considerable length of time before you find sufficient housing. You can extend your tent using a tarp and some branches to offer a sheltered area where you can cook or dry clothes.

- Wind-up AM/FM radio
- Mobile phone
- Wind-up charger
- Solar charger
- Gas mask
- Compact binoculars

Communication with the outside world can offer a lifeline. You never know who you may get through to or who is in a position to offer help during a disaster situation. While a gas mask may not be sufficient to protect you from radiation or biological agents it will be useful if you encounter police or military forces deploying tear gas or other crowd dispersal agents.

Being able to charge your electronic devices is vital as batteries can empty quickly. Only turn on your phone or radio when you need to as keeping these devices powered on will only waste power. Do not rely on a single source of power generation as you may need to charge batteries at night time which will render the solar charger useless.

- Paracord x15 metres (50 feet)
- Safety goggles
- Sunglasses
- Work gloves
- Rain poncho
- Toilet paper
- Candles x5

It may seem redundant to bring sunglasses with you, as you will be concerned with survival and not with looking cool while on the move, however, you may be marching in the direction of the sun all the time and sunglasses will offer you the ability to see clearly. If you are blinded by the sunshine you may stumble over the edge of a cliff or into another dangerous situation.

Minimising your exposure to dangerous situations is vital because there may not be any help available to you should you get badly cut or break a bone. You are on your own, stay safe.

- Clothing

This will depend on the climate conditions you are likely to face and the particular disaster that may have occurred. It is best if you pack enough clothing to stay warm enough to survive a potential drop in temperatures of up to 20^0C (68^0F). Clothes should be layered, with the outer garments being easy to remove and repack if necessary.

Bring two sets of clothes with you as this allows for one set to be washed and dried while you are wearing the other. Never stay in wet clothes for long as this will increase your potential exposure to hypothermia or pneumonia. If it is too warm where you are, remove other layers as soon as possible to reduce the risk of suffering from heat stroke.

Bring as many pairs of socks as you can fit and vary these between thick warm socks and light summer socks. If your feet are compromised by exposure to damp conditions, over too long a period of time, you will not be able to march effectively.

Disaster Dependent Supplies

Nuclear War

Red wine can help to reduce the body's absorption of radiation following a nuclear explosion. Bring a small bottle or red wine with you and drink this approximately 30 minutes after a nearby nuclear bomb detonation. This only slows down radiation absorption in the Thyroid gland. You should seek shelter from falling dust as soon as you can.

If you live in Ireland you should pack the anti-radiation iodine tablets, which were issued to you by the government in 2002 in the case of nuclear fallout, and take these according to the instructions on the pack. While your supply of anti-radiation iodine tablets will be out of date it is still better to have them with you.

A hand-held Geiger counter will be needed for checking the general radiation condition around you but also for checking water sources and any animals you trap for food. Should the levels be too high it is far better to abandon this new source of water or food and move on to another area.

Economic Collapse

You will need to pack bargaining supplies during an economic collapse such as Gold and Silver bullion. If this is not feasible you could pack things like crop seeds, toilet paper, high-end electronics or practical everyday items that you can trade for the supplies you will need.

If you are female you may consider packing as many condoms as possible as it may become necessary for you to trade sexual favours for supplies. Regardless of your current moral stance, things can change dramatically during a survival situation. Should you choose this route it is vital that you protect yourself at all times. Bring a pistol or knife with you during such encounters and take possession of the supplies you have agreed to trade **before** engaging in any sexual acts.

Chemical / Biological Warfare

A chemical protective suit complete with hood and boots can provide some protection, especially when combined with a suitable gas mask. While this is not a complete protective solution it should provide enough protection to escape any area affected by chemical or biological weapons.

If possible, pack as much plastic sheeting and duct tape as you can. With this, you may be able to create a sealed environment around your tent when you stop to rest for the night. Along with these supplies, you should also consider a portable air filter system as you should not stay in any air tight environment for an extended period of time.

Global Tsunami

This is the one disaster scenario where you will abandon your bug-out bag entirely. Attempting to run from an incoming tsunami wave while carrying your bug-out bag is a recipe for certain death. Leave your survival supplies at home and run for high ground as soon as you realise what is happening.

Pandemic

A chemical protective suit complete with hood and boots can provide some protection, especially when combined with a suitable gas mask. While this is not a complete protective solution it should provide enough protection to keep you out of harm's way from airborne diseases and from infection due to physical contact with infected people.

If possible, pack as much plastic sheeting and duct tape as you can. With this, you may be able to create a sealed environment around your tent when you stop to rest for the night. Along with these supplies, you should also consider a portable air filter system as you should not stay in any air tight environment for an extended period of time.

Personal hygiene will become even more important during a pandemic. With this in mind, you should pack extra soap and hand-sanitizer.

Alien Invasion

It is impossible to predict what, if any additional supplies would be needed for such a scenario. It may be necessary to go underground or into cave systems to avoid alien attack. Pack an extra length of para cord of 15 metres (50 feet) length as well as carabiners, harnesses and a crash helmet. These supplies would be needed if you were to scale a cliff in order to enter a cave or for potholing.

As you can see, there is a lot to pack so cut down on the size and weight of items as much as possible. Only select a backpack when you have all of your survival supplies ready. The backpack should not only provide enough space to carry all of your items but should also be comfortable to carry when fully loaded. Search for a backpack that provides extra padding in the shoulder straps and support for the back. Avoid gear bags or any other bag that requires you to carry it in your hands, only buy a backpack that will go over your shoulders as you will most likely need both hands available at all times while on the move.

When packing your bug-out bag ensure that the items you are less likely to use, such as spare hiking boots, rope, tent, etc. are packed at the bottom of the bag. Items such as water, axe, knife, etc. should be at the top of your bag, for easy retrieval.

Spend some time researching your local area to determine where you will run to, where are the best sources of water such as streams or external water taps, where can you set up your tent for the night where it won't be seen by others. Do not rely on one single location to run to, you must keep your options open as you don't know what that location will be like during an emergency, perhaps large groups of people are evacuating a city on the route where you planned on going, making it unsafe.

How many people are in your family? You will need to have bug-out bags for them too. It may seem like far too much for you to carry but after 3 days your water supply will be all but gone and water is very heavy. As you consume items from your bug-out bag you will be able to move further due to the decrease in weight that you need to carry.

When using your bug-out supplies it is important to conserve as much as possible and impose self-rationing on your food and water. To conserve battery power you can bring wind-up devices which can be recharged easily.

Once you have packed the above supplies, and if you have any space remaining, it is strongly advised to fill the remaining space with extra water and food.

Water

Most people take the supply of water for granted. Let's face it, if you want water you just go to the tap and turn it on, or grab a bottle that you bought from a shop. But what if disaster struck right now and you went to the tap only to discover that it doesn't work anymore and it will never work again. What if you had just run out of bottled water on the same day? What would you do? In 3 days, without water, you will die. Where are you going to get water from?

Water should always be considered your number one priority, above anything else. If you haven't previously prepared a stock of water and find yourself in a difficult shortage you can always find water in the cisterns of toilets. This water must be boiled and filtered before drinking. There may be a tap outside your home that is not connected to the same supply as your house and this should be checked as soon as possible to see if it works. It is possible that a small amount of water is trapped in the gutters on your roof. If you can get to these extract as much water as possible. Some brand new, clean sponges and a bucket are great for gathering such small amounts of water.

If you need to bug-out make sure that you take note of any potential water sources that you find. You might come across a stream or abandoned house with a working tap. Any water you gather must be boiled and filtered before drinking. In the event of Nuclear War, you should check any potential water sources with your Geiger counter to assess radiation levels.

Always aim for consuming up to 2 litres (4.2 pints) of water each day. Should you find yourself in danger of running out of water and cannot get access to more you should begin rationing immediately. When rationing, only drink water when you absolutely have to and drink a tiny amount, just enough to wet your lips. When rationing water it is important to cut down on your physical exertion as this uses a lot of the body's stored reserves.

Should you be deprived of water for long enough you will begin to suffer from dehydration which shows symptoms of dizziness, sluggishness and confusion. If you begin to suffer from these symptoms it is vital that you dramatically increase your intake of water. If you can't find water soon you will die.

When establishing a permanent base you should find an area with a nearby stream as this will provide a plentiful supply of water. Do not become complacent with this new water supply. All water should be boiled and filtered before consumption, even if the stream looks crystal clear.

If there is any advanced warning of an impending disaster you should fill as many containers as possible with water. Even if you need to leave your home because of the disaster it is better to have this water gathered than to not have any available.

Another way to sterilise water is by using bleach if you have any available. Add 2 small drops of bleach for every 1 litre (2.1 pints) of water. Stir this mixture thoroughly and leave to stand for at least 30 minutes before drinking.

Avoid drinking sea water at all costs as this will kill you, even small amounts of sea water have been known to kill quickly.

Rainwater should be perfectly safe to drink without boiling or filtering unless you are facing one of the following emergencies:

- Nuclear War
- Super Volcano
- Asteroid Strike
- Chemical / Biological Warfare
- Pandemic
- Alien Invasion

A great way to collect very large amounts of rainwater is to tie up a large tarp to some trees or other structure by the corners of the tarp. Ensure the tarp is sloping downwards slightly and forming a "V" shape. All rain that falls on the tarp will be diverted into the "V" shape and ultimately channelled into a container.

Any water you collect should be kept indoors and out of direct sunlight as this can cause algae to propagate in the water.

Food

Without food, you will die within 30-40 days. Almost every large department store will only have enough food in stock for 3 days, under normal selling conditions, and this food will be looted within hours of any emergency situation.

It is vital, for your ongoing survival, to ensure that you have a large stockpile of food and the ability to grow your own food should this become necessary.

Different types of emergencies will see different levels of the availability of food. Whatever you are prepping for it will most likely become necessary, at some stage, for you to gather, grow, or loot more food.

Nuclear War

Following a global thermo-nuclear war the availability of food will drop to non-existent. You will not be able to buy food in shops, local farmers will barely be able to provide food for their own family, yet alone be able to provide for the general populous.

It will be up to you to source your own supply of food. This will become very difficult as mass looting will have emptied shelves. Growing food will be hazardous as the soil will be irradiated and hunting animals for food will also present dangers from radiation as this will be absorbed through the skin of the animal as well as from and food or water that the animal has consumed.

Economic Collapse

This is a strange scenario as there will be more than enough food but you will not be able to afford to buy any. You may need to resort to soup kitchens or other emergency supplies during this time but be warned, you will only be given a small amount of food that will not be enough for your basic daily needs.

Attempt to grow food if possible. This carries further dangers as your crops may be looted. If you have a very secure back garden it may be possible to grow food without it being interfered with. Another option would be to grow as much as possible indoors.

Prepare to go hungry for long periods of time during a global economic collapse.

Super Volcano

Following a super volcano eruption, the global food supplies will dwindle for several years as nuclear winter, brought on by the ash cloud obscuring sunlight, will cause crops to fail.

Expect food prices to soar to record highs. Wherever possible, try to grow your own food and store as much as you can.

Asteroid Strike

This scenario depends on the size, composition, speed, angle of attack and the location where the asteroid strikes but will most likely result in a dramatic failure of crops within the first 4 years of the strike.

Food will be in very limited supply. You may not be able to rely on soup kitchens or other emergency food distribution due to the widespread destruction of infrastructure.

Chemical / Biological Warfare

This should not have any major impact on food production but will have an impact on the distribution of food. As with any war, transport will become dangerous and result in late shipments of food to local distribution centres and shops or will result in some shipments simply not arriving.

Expect sporadic shortages but generally, there should be enough food to go round. When shops are fully stocked take full advantage of this and buy as much food as possible so that you can build up a reliable stockpile.

Global Tsunami

While some agricultural areas will be destroyed, resulting in an end to food production in those areas, it should not have a major impact on your ability to get food. The destruction of agricultural land will be offset by the sheer amount of people that will be killed during this event.

The fewer people there are, the more food there will be for everyone else. If you are having difficulty finding food after this disaster you will find a ready supply the further inland you travel.

Planet X

Just like the Nuclear War scenario above, Planet X will potentially result in mass food shortages, an inability to grow food, and mass looting events.

It is best if you can attempt to grow your own food, in any place that you can; on land, indoors or on water. There may be a bunker in your town or city, either for your local government or maintained by your local civil defence organisation. These bunkers will have food but not a lot. If you can, get to one of these locations and take as much as you can carry, but be warned; these bunkers will be heavily defended.

Solar Flare / EMP

As with an Economic Collapse, there will be plenty of food available. The only problem will be an inability to deliver that food to cities or towns. All vehicles will stop working during and after this event.

If you are in a city or town you will need to migrate to the countryside in order to buy food from a local farmer. If you want to make some money during this time you can always set up a distribution company, delivering food to cities using a horse and cart.

Global Quake

While this event will certainly slow down the harvesting and distribution of food, it will most likely only affect a single growing season.

Should you already have a large stockpile of food available than you may not even be affected by this slight interruption to the food supply. However, if you have not prepared in advance then you will definitely go hungry and will stay hungry for anything up to 6 months before food production and delivery networks can get back on track.

Pandemic

As a pandemic will only affect humans, and some animals, there will be nothing wrong with food production or distribution, however, the problems will arise when farmers and delivery drivers succumb to the virus. Expect food production to slow down dramatically for the duration of the pandemic.

Do not rely on soup kitchens or other emergency distribution as these places may be filled with the infected, thus increasing your chances of contracting the virus. The less you expose yourself to other people, the better chance you have of surviving.

If possible, grow your own crops in your back garden. These crops should remain fairly secure as others will not run the risk of becoming infected by going outside.

Global Famine

Having a large and secure stockpile of food is vital during a Global Famine event as crops will not grow properly during this time. The famine will not last very long but it will most likely last long enough to exhaust your stockpile of food. You should implement rationing as early as possible to avoid running out of food.

Alien Invasion

This scenario is the great unknown but I would believe that all food production and distribution would cease within the first 24-hours of the beginning of this event.

Growing your own food may not be possible as a ground invasion will follow the initial bombardment of the planet. The only survivable option is to have a large stockpile of food available to you.

Preserving food

Food has been successfully preserved since the dawn of civilisation without the need for modern chemicals. During ancient Roman times, salt was used for preserving meat so much that salt became an alternative currency.

Large quantities of salt will draw water out of meat. Water is required by all living things in order to grow so when salt removes water from meat it stops all growing processes, including stopping the decomposition of meat. Salt is also toxic to microbes resulting in meat that has a dramatic decrease in its ability to make you sick.

Another method of preserving meat is to smoke it or extreme drying of the meat. Any fresh meat you gather should be rubbed heavily in salt and hung in a cool dry room, away from direct sunlight.

As food will become a valuable resource it is best if you keep your food production, stockpiling and preservation methods a closely guarded secret. Smoking or even cooking food can draw the attention of people who are desperately hungry. They will kill you for your supplies.

If you have vacuum packing equipment you can seal cuts of meat. Vacuum sealing can lead to meat lasting 3-5 times longer compared to normal storage. This method is best used if you have a steady supply of electricity from solar or wind turbines and are able to run a freezer as a result. Never store meat in a freezer without it being wrapped in plastic as the meat will suffer greatly from frostbite by being directly exposed to ice crystals.

One of the easiest foods to preserve is rice. This should be kept in Mylar bags along with an oxygen absorbing capsule. Vacuum seal the Mylar bags with each bag being small enough that, once opened it can be consumed in a few days. While unadvised, you can survive on rice alone for the rest of your days if needed.

The following is a list of foods that can last forever if stored correctly:

- Honey
- Rice
- Sugar
- Maple syrup
- Vanilla extract
- Distilled white vinegar
- Salt
- Corn-starch

Archaeologists, excavating the Great Pyramids in Egypt, have discovered 3,000 years old jars of honey that are still edible.

Growing Food

While it is beyond the scope of this book to teach you how to grow food, the following is a list of food stuff that can be easily grown and are perfect for long-term survival situations. A lot of the foods listed below can, in the correct conditions and with the correct equipment, be grown indoors.

- Artichokes
- Beans
- Beetroot
- Cabbage
- Carrots
- Cassava
- Corn
- Garlic
- Kale
- Onions
- Potatoes
- Radish
- Squash
- Sweet Peas
- Sweet Potatoes
- Tomatoes

Hunting

Hunting animals as a source of food and for their pelts will prove an invaluable skill after certain disasters; however, hunting is not something that can be picked up overnight. You will need to practice your hunting skills as much as possible.

Remember that when you are using your cunning against another animal, they are using their cunning to either evade or hunt you. If you run into the woods, firing a weapon on full-auto while screaming at the top of your lungs, your gun-hoe attitude will only succeed in scaring off **all** potential dinners. The biggest skills to learn when hunting are stealth and infinite patience. When hunting, you could be away from your shelter and stalking an animal for hours on end.

If you are using a rifle to hunt, be warned that you may only have one shot. As soon as you fire, any animal within range of the sound will scatter and may not return for hours or days. The best weapons to use when hunting are archery bow, crossbow or knife as these weapons have a low noise level. Even if you miss you will still have animals in the area as they will not scatter from the noise of gunfire. Always try to collect any used arrows as you may find yourself running out at some stage in the future.

The best way for you to perfect hunting techniques is to learn as much as you can from other hunters. If you are lucky enough to have a friend or family member who regularly hunts you may want to join them. There may be a hunting club in your local area that would be glad to have you as a member and teach you.

During the following emergencies it may be hazardous to eat any animals you kill due to radiation absorption or poisoning:

- Nuclear War
- Super Volcano
- Asteroid Strike
- Chemical / Biological Warfare
- Pandemic
- Alien Invasion

Never eat an animal that is already dead when you find it, as you don't know what could have killed it. Eating such an animal could introduce harmful pathogens into your system and render you extremely ill or, in a worst-case scenario, could kill you.

Carefully observe any potential kill as the animal may be drinking from a tainted stream or river. This animal may be very ill and make you sick as a result. If the animal looks healthy, is fast on his feet and seems to retain a high level of awareness it should be ok to eat.

You will need a strong stomach when it comes to hunting and preparing the catch in order to eat it. Do you have what it takes to cut the head off an animal? Maintaining a strong constitution during emergency times is vital in order to successfully survive.

Any traps or snares that you set should be dismantled at the end of the hunt in case it causes damage to any human passing through the area.

Avoid hunting the following animals as they prove very difficult to successfully hunt and kill or may be far too dangerous:

- Bears
- Buffalo
- Coyote
- Crocodiles
- Elk
- Hippopotamus
- Lions
- Moose
- Mountain Goats
- Mountain Lion
- Rhinoceros
- Whitetail Deer
- Wild Boar
- Wild Dogs
- Wild Turkey
- Wolf
- Zebra

Never approach a wounded animal as this is the time they will launch a ferocious attack in order to defend themselves. Any animal with horns or other defensive weapons has the capacity to cause an incredible amount of damage to you if they decide to charge. When hunting, always expect the unexpected and be prepared to escape the area if needed.

Fishing

If you have never been fishing before then don't worry, it doesn't need to be a complex endeavour with lots of very expensive equipment. A simple net and a shallow stream can quickly and easily result in a catch if the stream has a lot of fish. Setting a net in the stream and anchoring it on the banks can result in a large catch over a number of hours. This net should be monitored at all times in case the volume of fish in the net threatens to pull it from its moorings.

If you are near a Salmon spawning ground you will see fish leaping out of the water in order to navigate natural obstacles. Bears will often wait in these areas and catch fish as they jump out of the water.

If you go down the traditional route of having a fishing rod you can place multiple hooks on the line to increase the possibility of catching a fish or even multiple fish at one time. In order to catch worms for the hooks, you can use a basin of slightly soapy water and drop this into grass or mud and wait. As the soapy solution is absorbed into the earth the worms will try to escape by coming to the surface. As they break through just grab them and place in a container. Don't worry, any soapy solution that is absorbed by the worms will be minimal and will not affect the fish that is caught.

To ensure that you are fishing in a stream or river with healthy fish you should look for green plants growing on both banks of the river. If there is nothing growing here, or the plants look dead or dying you should assume that anything caught from this river will be toxic. Dead fish floating in the water or lying on the bank is also a danger sign that you should not eat anything from this river, or use it as a water source.

It is important that fish are prepared properly before cooking as there is a high risk of choking. Remove all scales, internal organs, head, tail, fins and small bones.

Disaster Myths

Nuclear War

One of the biggest myths is that a global thermo-nuclear war would cause such vast levels of destruction that it would render Earth an uninhabitable rock where nothing will survive, not even bacteria. This couldn't be further from the truth. All nuclear weapons are pointed at targets of interest, such as power plants, military installations, airports and cities. While these areas will certainly be destroyed, there will be vast areas of countryside unaffected by the blasts. Some countries may not even experience radioactive fallout, depending on the prevailing winds, such as; Papua New Guinea, Indonesia, Bolivia, most of Brazil and most of the African continent, as these countries do not possess any viable targets. The rule of thumb is that most countries in the Northern Hemisphere will be targeted.

Another myth is that a single nuclear weapon could vaporise an entire city like London or Paris. This is not true; in fact, it would take several weapons to cause enough destruction to classify such a large city as vaporised.

Nuclear fallout will kill everyone and render the entire atmosphere and land unusable. This is false. Nuclear fallout will begin to rain down on Earth approximately 30 minutes after a nuclear explosion and could affect an area close to the explosion. This radioactive fallout will usually not be too harmful if exposed to the skin for a short time but will prove deadly if inhaled. People inside bunkers should be safe from fallout and the radioactive effects will dissipate within 2 weeks to 1 month to levels that are not too harmful to humans. Within 1 to 2 years after a global thermonuclear war radioactive fallout should be fully dissipated.

Economic Collapse

The biggest myth would be that the entire planet's infrastructure, factories, farms, business's etc. would immediately fail and send society back to the Stone Age. This is not true. Many businesses and factories will continue to operate as normal but the vast majority would fail, leaving potentially billions of people out of work overnight. It will be this mass unemployment that will fuel the great hardships to come.

Without a job, it will become increasingly difficult to look after yourself or provide for your family. The small percentage of people left in employment will not be able to sustain social services, which in turn will collapse. Those who still have a job after the collapse will see massive increases in income tax while countries try their best to stay solvent.

Super Volcano

Some people believe that if a super volcano was to erupt it would spew lava across the entire surface of Earth and destroy everything in its path. While lava will be released during such an eruption it will not affect anything beyond 65km (40 miles) from the centre of the eruption. A devastating amount of ash will cover a wider area that could extend up to 500km (311 miles) in diameter.

Another myth about super volcano eruptions is that the ash cloud generated will be so thick and dense that it will envelop the entire planet and people will suffocate. Again, not true. While there will be a major risk from the ash cloud, it will come in the form of environmental changes due to a decrease in light reaching the surface of

Earth and there will be great risk to aircraft, which cannot fly through volcanic ash without sustaining damage to the engines. When the Eyjafjallajökull volcano in Iceland erupted in 2010 the ash cloud was so large that it caused aircraft to be grounded across most of Europe which lasted, intermittently, for several weeks.

Poisonous gas from the super volcano will suffocate every living thing on Earth within a matter of hours! While there will be poisonous gas released during the eruption it will dissipate quickly and will only affect an area that is so close to the actual eruption itself that you would most likely be killed before the gas can reach you.

Asteroid Strike

Asteroids are highly radioactive and will irradiate the planet after a strike! While some minerals contained in asteroids may be radioactive, they will be no more radioactive than any standard rock in your garden. Don't concern yourself with radioactive fallout from the asteroid.

NASA will come to our rescue if a gigantic asteroid should threaten Earth. Not true.

While NASA and other space agencies are working on plans to stop such strikes, at this time, it is impossible for any of the current plans to work. In fact, most large asteroids are detected only a few days from Earth or after they pass us by.

Asteroids need to be nuked from the inside, like in the movies! While there is an advantage to be gained from blowing up an asteroid using a nuclear warhead that is buried deep in the core, this would not be necessary. An asteroid could easily be blown to pieces by nuclear weapons detonating on the surface; however, nuclear weapons are designed to be fired from one location on Earth to another, usually targeted by GPS coordinates. If a nation decides to launch its weapons into space it will be very difficult for them to successfully target and hit the asteroid. The likelihood of nuclear weapons succeeding is, therefore, unlikely.

Chemical / Biological Warfare

Chemical or biological agents will be deployed in missiles to rain down on cities. This is untrue. It has been shown in the past that missiles are very ineffective for such use as most of the agent will be destroyed due to atmospheric pressures and the surviving agent would need to be deployed in a very precise air-burst that is technically impossible to achieve.

You will be able to see the gas cloud and be able to outrun it! Most, if not all, military agents are colourless and odourless. The first indication that one of these agents is present is when people begin to suffer the devastating effects of exposure.

Terrorist can easily produce their own biological weapons in a garden shed. It takes advanced laboratories and expert scientists to create such agents. The biggest risk from terrorists is if they can get their hands on agents that have already been created in a military lab.

Global Tsunami

The entirety of Earth's surface will be washed away by a single giant wave of biblical proportions! This couldn't be further from the truth. Tsunamis come in several waves over a period of a few hours, but like all waves, they only wash up on the shore. During a global tsunami event, it is possible that all coastlines are badly affected but inland regions would survive.

A global tsunami event will see waves that are hundreds of meters tall hitting coastlines. While there could be some regions that experience these mega tsunamis, most regions will see waves of only a metre or two in size sweeping inland.

Planet X

The government will tell us if they detect this planet entering our Solar System. They won't. Should this planet exist and if it does enter our Solar System, which could cause extreme cataclysm on Earth, all governments will be sworn to secrecy in order to prevent mass panic among the 7 billion of us on Earth. They will say nothing and hope that nobody will notice.

Planet X inhabitants will fly over to Earth and take over, while it passes through our Solar System! If Planet X exists and if it is inhabited by intelligent aliens, they would not survive on their own planet for very long. It is believed that Planet X is in a highly elliptical orbit which means at its farthest from us it will be far beyond Pluto. Not enough sunlight would be available on this planet for thousands of years and any intelligent life would have an impossible time surviving. Even if there are intelligent creatures on Planet X, as it passes through our Solar System they will also be experiencing catastrophic problems on their planet which would make it unfeasible to launch a mission to Earth.

Solar Flare / EMP

We will be able to recover full electrical power within a matter of weeks! In reality, it will take a very long time to recover. Remember, that all electrical transformers, sub-stations, etc. will be destroyed. These will need to be rebuilt in a time when nothing electrical or electronic can be built.

All I need to do is turn off my electronic devices and they will survive. For that to happen you would require advanced warning of such an event, which is most likely not going to come. Even if you do switch off your devices they will still be damaged, not to the extent they would be if they were switched on at the time, but they would still suffer damage.

A massive EMP event will cause people to drop from massive electrocutions as if they were struck by lightning. Not true. This event will not act like lightning and will not produce any lightning. It would have no effect on you whatsoever unless the unlikely event occurs where an electrical or electronic device that you are touching at the time was to generate a massive electrical overload that travelled into you.

A massive solar flare will only affect the side of Earth that it hits! When a solar flare hits Earth it will disrupt the entire magnetic field, which surrounds our planet.

A massive solar flare, that can shut down electrical grids, has never happened before so why should I bother preparing for it? It has happened before. In 1989 a solar flare hit Earth and shut down the entire electrical grid in Quebec, Canada. The effect was so prominent that the electrical grid failed in only 1.5 minutes.

Global Quake

The entire surface of Earth will shake at the same time! While a global quake will be devastating over a short period of time, it will most likely be caused by a series of earthquakes that occur over a period of maybe 1 month. You will see earthquakes of varying magnitudes strike in different parts of the planet during this time. There could be multiple earthquakes in a single day but generally, this event will be spread out over a period of time.

All buildings will collapse during a global quake. This is not true. Most modern buildings, especially in earthquake prone zones are designed to withstand very large earthquakes. Even modern buildings that are not designed to withstand earthquakes, because they are not built in danger zones, will still be able to withstand earthquakes. The biggest loss would be in third world countries where buildings are constructed with antiquated technologies, materials and practices.

Pandemic

A pandemic cannot occur in modern times because the CDC and W.H.O. (World Health Organisation) will easily contain the problem. While it is possible for us to contain a virus and impose quarantines our modern society of globalisation means that it is even easier for a pandemic to occur due to the frequency and volume of international flights and the scale of our cargo transportation network. By the time a dangerous virus is identified and quarantines are enforced it may already be too late to stop it.

The CDC will save the day! No, they won't. While they provide invaluable services to prevent the spread of a deadly outbreak they are unable to stop it's spread. The only thing they can do is slow down the spread of the virus and hopefully, come up with a way to combat the problem. It is more likely that the virus itself will spread until it cannot spread any further, only then will you see a massive decrease in new infections and deaths as a result of the virus. Nature will be the one who saves the day.

Global Famine

There will be no more food left or growing in the world, we're all doomed! While a global famine will result in many hundreds of millions of people dying of starvation and malnutrition it certainly will not be because food no longer exists. There will be plenty of areas on Earth that will continue to be capable of food production. The problems of such a scenario will revolve around the fact that food production will slow down dramatically. As it stands, there is more than enough food growing on Earth to feed everyone, we routinely throw away many thousands of tonnes of food each day. It will be the lack of availability of food for a short period of time that will cause most of the deaths. Should we lose a single season of crops across the world at one time; most will die within 1 month.

Famines cannot be predicted and this event will come as a big surprise to the world. This is not true. There are plenty of tools and models to effectively predict future problems with food supplies. Whether your government releases this information to you is the real problem. Most likely, you will only hear about food shortages when it has already happened.

The planet is vastly overpopulated and a global food shortage is guaranteed to happen at any moment if nothing is done to cull the population. This is complete nonsense. Scientists believe that the maximum population, where food is concerned, is 10 billion people. We have a long way to go before we reach those levels.

Alien Invasion

This one is far more difficult to outline possible myths because such an event has not occurred in recorded history, but we can look at some things that occur in popular movies about this scenario.

We will discover some weakness of the alien's technology and once we exploit this weakness they will be easily defeated within a few hours. If they are intelligent enough to create interstellar ships to conquer Earth and have presumably attacked other planets in the past than they are smart enough to think of and correct any vulnerabilities.

A common cold will eventually kill the aliens! No, it won't. They will have already identified any pathogens with the potential to cause them damage and formulated an effective vaccine. They wouldn't come here if they couldn't survive here.

Dangers

Apart from the obvious dangers that you will face during a disaster, such as the event itself, there are other dangers that many will not consider dangers or will not prepare for. People can get desperate to ensure their own survival. Military forces can be ordered to fire on civilians. If the disaster is bad enough you could even find yourself being rounded-up for orderly disposal.

Military and Police Forces

During the following emergencies it is best if you avoid the military or police forces as they could prove deadly:

- Nuclear War
- Chemical / Biological Warfare
- Planet X
- Solar Flare / EMP
- Pandemic

Other people

During emergency situations, people will become very desperate for supplies and for their own continued survival. Expect people, who are ordinarily docile, to turn deadly. Always remain on high alert when dealing with people you encounter either during a disaster or afterwards.

Imagine today's society where there are people who are capable of killing you in order to rob your belongings. You don't encounter these people every day and usually only hear about them through news reports. You're always wary of dark alleys and other areas where you may encounter these people but you can always avoid these areas and find safe places. Usually shopping centres, bars or other places where people gather. You know that there is safety in numbers because the majority of people are peaceful and not interested in putting you in danger. But what if that situation was reversed and now most people were out to get you?

During the following disasters it is best to avoid contact with other people wherever possible:

- Nuclear War
- Super Volcano
- Asteroid Strike
- Planet X
- Solar Flare / EMP
- Pandemic

Wild Animals

If you need to bug-out following an emergency and need to trek through wilderness you may encounter wild animals that could vigorously defend their territory. Even if you stay in a city or town you could encounter packs of domestic dogs. When dogs gather in packs it can become very dangerous for you.

If you do encounter a wild animal it is best to back off and walk away from their territory in the direction you came. Find another route that will take you around that animal and his territory. Most wild animals will try to avoid a fight. By backing away from their territory you stand the greatest chance of survival. Wild animals will only attack when they feel that they have no other option left. While backing away keep as calm as possible as animals can smell fear which can lead them to believe that you are so weak they could take you as food. By remaining perfectly calm you will give the impression that you are, at least, as dominant as the animal and you should not be attacked.

Unseen dangers

A survivalist mindset is not only about preparing for those things that you can foresee but also being prepared to react to the unknown dangers that you may encounter.

As a prepper, you should always be prepared to abandon everything that you have tirelessly gathered and stockpiled if you need to. Think of all those people who would stay in their homes during a disaster. They are tied to the one place because they feel safe there and all of their processions are there. Your life and the life of your family will always be more valuable than any house or materialistic thing.

Always stay on alert for the unseen and be prepared to abandon everything, run until your lungs feel like they are going to explode or kill if necessary.

Weapons

During the following disasters, it is vital that you are not only properly prepared, but also properly armed.

- Nuclear War
- Asteroid Strike
- Planet X
- Global Quake
- Pandemic
- Alien Invasion

During these events, you are at risk from military, police forces and desperate civilians who will do anything necessary to protect themselves and potentially kill you to get their hands on your supplies.

During the aftermath of hurricane Katrina, which struck New Orleans in 2005, there were reports of people in high-rise buildings shooting people on the street who were trying to flee the city. These snipers were ordinary citizens who, in some cases, believed that they were witnessing the apocalypse and were randomly targeting people. Hurricane Katrina was just a storm that affected a tiny region on Earth; imagine what things would be like during a global thermo-nuclear War.

Guns

Guns may not be readily available to you. If you live in Ireland or England you need to apply for a licence to own a firearm and this process could take up to a year to complete. In some cases, these licences are reviewed at intervals to determine if you qualify to keep the weapon. These strict laws mean that if you get advanced warning of an impending disaster you may not have time to acquire a gun.

Identify your local gun shop and be prepared to loot this shop if necessary, but be warned that a lot of other desperate people will be looting this shop at the same time. Things could get deadly very quickly. The owners of the gun shop may take up positions within the building to fend off looters. If you do manage to safely enter the gun shop you will still need to gain access to the safe room where the weapons and ammunition are kept. This will be a very difficult undertaking.

If, on the other hand, you live in America or any other country with relaxed gun ownership laws you can easily begin stocking up on weapons and ammunition now.

You do not need to own countless guns as you will only be able to carry 1 or 2 at any one time. Invest your money in the most reliable weapon possible that takes the most common calibre or ammunition. A very reliable weapon is the Russian-made **Kalashnikov AK-47** assault rifle. These weapons do not require constant cleaning and rarely jam.

If you are living in Ireland or England and manage to acquire a gun licence you will now be faced with the difficulty of storing ammunition. There are strict laws in place to ensure that the amount of ammunition you can purchase at any one time or store is very limited. If you do manage to exceed this amount expect a call from your local firearms police inspector. If however, the purchasing and storing of ammunition does not come with limits the best amount to store is ... as much as you can. You should never need to worry about ammunition conservation if planning for one of the above disaster scenarios.

You may believe that it will be very easy for you to kill any threat that comes your way; however firing a weapon in anger against another human being is a very difficult thing to do. Armed police forces and soldiers are heavily trained to fight their natural instincts to preserve life. Killing another human being is not an easy thing to do. You will be experiencing large amounts of fear and guilt while attacking the individual. A psychological phenomenon will occur where you believe that if you just stop the attack and drop your weapon, that your attacker will leave you alone. They won't, you need to fight through these psychological pressures and learn to fire your weapon before you are killed by your attacker.

When firing on your attacker it is best to shoot at the main trunk of the body. Do not try to be creative and go for a headshot or a limb (if you are trying to slow down your target and not kill them) as you will most likely miss. Fire 2 rounds into the torso and back-off by at least 10 metres (32 feet). If your enemy is still moving after you back-off, fire 2 more rounds into the torso and run. Don't wait around to see if they are dead or not, they may have friends in hiding who are about to attack or they may be ahead of another group that will be on your position in a few minutes. Run for cover, wait a few minutes to see if there are more threats, then run again. Do this until you are very far away from the attack location.

The best possible stance to take is one of stealth and evasion. If you don't ever need to fire your weapon you stand a bigger chance of survival. Don't intentionally face-off against another person unless you absolutely have to. If you can avoid a confrontation, even if this takes you many kilometres out of your intended route you will live to fight another day.

Other Weapons

If you live in a country with strict gun laws you can still get your hands on effective weapons such as;

- Compound archery bow
- Compound crossbow
- Sword
- Javelin
- Knives and Axes

A good quality archery bow can become a very effective medium-range weapon if you have no other weaponry options. These can be purchased from most good sports stores and usually do not require additional state licencing. A compound bow or compound crossbow is best because their construction provides additional power to the arrow when it is fired. Don't buy cheap equipment; the more you invest the more likely it is that your weapon will last effectively for decades. To prepare the weapon for a disaster scenario you should buy extra string, parts and as many arrows as you can. Take professional archery lessons and master the skill of using this weapon. **NOTE:** At the time of writing, if you live in Ireland it is illegal for you to own a crossbow without a valid firearms certificate.

Some good close quarter combat weapons are swords, axes and knives. It takes far more nerves of steel to fight with these weapons as opposed to a gun or crossbow, which can be used from a distance. If you purchase a javelin to use as a spear, it is best if you learn how to fight with this as a close-quarters weapon. Don't throw it at your attacker as you will only have one shot and will most likely miss. **NOTE:** At the time of writing, if you live in Ireland it is illegal for you to own a sword and you will not find any for sale in shops.

If you do find yourself engaged in hand-to-hand combat be aware that this will be a fight to the death. There will be no giving up and no time-outs. You may be fighting for not only your own life but for the lives of your loved ones or kids. The only winner will be the one who is still alive at the end of the fight. Many people believe that they could easily do this but these kinds of fights will be unlike anything you have ever experienced and, contrary to what you see in the movies, these fights usually only last a few seconds to a minute at the most.

Shelter

You may be able to either stay in or return to your home if faced with the following emergencies:

- Economic Collapse
- Super Volcano
- Asteroid Strike
- Chemical / Biological Warfare
- Global Tsunami
- Solar Flare / EMP
- Global Quake
- Pandemic
- Global Famine

If you live in any form of an urban area, town or city, it may prove vital to leave as soon as disaster strikes. Depending on the disaster you might be able to return to your home, but what if the disaster wipes out your city? Where will you go?

If you face a nuclear war and your house survives undamaged expect the authorities to house as many displaced people as possible in your home. You will not be given a choice about this and could be subject to robberies and attacks from your new tenants.

Temporary shelters

While you are in the process of bugging-out you will find yourself living in a tent, possibly in cold and dangerous conditions. This type of shelter is not designed for long-term survival and over time you can become susceptible to infections, disease or suffer the effects of exposure.

If you don't have a secure location to escape to you should always keep an eye out for any abandoned buildings that could prove to be an adequate shelter. Many people take their houses for granted; they will pass homeless people on the street without much consideration of how they are surviving or the hardships that they endure. Your house is a very precious commodity and you will only truly appreciate it when you are faced with living in the wild when you are cold, hungry and exposed to the elements.

Underground Shelters

During the following disasters it will become vital that you find adequate shelter in an underground location:

- Nuclear War
- Super Volcano (depending on your location)
- Asteroid Attack (depending on your location)
- Planet X
- Alien Invasion

Underground shelters can range from the basement in your home to a cave. Staying underground has the added benefit of a constant temperature without any extremes of hot or cold.

Contrary to popular belief an underground bunker will not protect you from a direct strike from a nuclear weapon. While the bunker itself may survive such a blast it will definitely be sealed due to rubble. If your air supply was to survive this you will find yourself trapped underground with no possible way of digging yourself out. Do not create a fortified bunker in any urban environment; instead create one far out in the countryside.

The best possible location for any form of bunker or safe house is in an area that is extremely difficult for you to reach. If it is difficult for you to get there it will be difficult for others to find you and steal your survival supplies.

If you want to ride out any form of emergency in an underground bunker you will need enough supplies to last at least 5 years. After this time things may have settled down enough on the surface to safely permit you going outside.

As with all things prepper related it is best if you keep the location of any bunkers a closely guarded secret and only pay for materials or labour with cash. If the military discovers that you have a bunker it may be taken over or raided following a disaster.

Houses

A basic house or even a cabin in the woods will provide enough shelter to live comfortably following a disaster. The only thing to consider is *location*, *location*, *location*. Where is your bug-out house? Could it be in the range of a tsunami, nuclear strike or on a fault line? If you are planning to purchase a special bug-out house you will need to consider these things carefully. You will also need to consider if migrations of people could pass through the area at some stage in the future.

Where will you get fresh water from? A house by a strong stream sounds like a good idea. What raw materials exist around the house? If you get a cabin in the woods you may have an indefinite supply of firewood.

Think very carefully before settling for a location to stay. You may find yourself there for the rest of your life.

Starting a Fire

Your ability to start a fire can mean the difference between life and death. This ability will become necessary during the following emergencies or temporarily should you find yourself bugging out for more than 12 hours:

- Nuclear War
- Economic Collapse
- Planet X
- Solar Flare / EMP
- Alien Invasion

During these emergencies, you may never return to having fire supplied by gas or other easy means and will need to learn how to manually create a fire from limited supplies. Despite being in emergency conditions you should still maintain a sense of safety. If you are in a wooded area, don't just randomly start a fire as you could find yourself caught up in a very dangerous wildfire situation. Clear an area for the fire and place rocks around the perimeter of the fire to ensure that it is kept under control. Never leave a fire unattended for any reason and always extinguish a fire with dirt or sand if available.

The main components of starting a fire are:

- Ignition source
- Kindling
- Fuel

Without an ignition source, you will never be able to start a fire. Kindling is tiny pieces of flammable materials that will catch fire easily and the fuel is things such as; large pieces or wood, coal, etc.

A very easy way to start a fire is to use some form of accelerant such as petrol or fire-lighters. If you have these in abundance, and butane lighters or some matches you could have more of an ability to light a fire than most people who are caught up in a disaster and are unprepared.

Never add too much fuel to a fire too quickly. If you manage to start a small fire and suddenly dump a bag of coal on it or several large pieces of wood you run the risk of smothering the fire. It is best if you add fuel slowly until there is a raging fire.

If you do not have any butane lighters or matches you can start a fire from other materials in your bug-out-bag such as; magnifying glass (if it is a sunny day) or a flint lighter.

The last option available to you is to start a fire by hand. We've seen this method being performed in countless movies and TV shows, where a stick is used and rubbed between the hands vigorously to heat up another piece of wood, hot enough to light kindling. To start a fire this way, first ensure that all materials are bone dry and find a piece of wood that is split or has a natural depression in it, possibly from a knot that has fallen out. Using a knife sharpen another piece of wood, this will be the piece that you rub together in your hands. Add some small amounts of kindling or wool fibres to the depression and use the sharpened piece of wood to create enough friction in the depression that it heats up, and eventually sets fire to, the kindling.

Once the fire is burning bright enough you can begin to slowly add more fuel.

Healthcare and First Aid

When it comes to first aid it is best if you are professionally trained to deal with injuries. It simply would not be enough to describe techniques and procedures to you in a book. One of the best places to learn basic first aid is through your local Civil Defence group. They are always happy to receive new volunteers and will gladly teach you lifesaving skills for free. You can expand this training later by paying for advanced classes.

During the following emergencies, the health care system will be far too overwhelmed to be in a position to treat you and it may prove life-threatening for you to approach a hospital:

- Nuclear War
- Super Volcano
- Asteroid Strike
- Chemical / Biological Warfare
- Planet X
- Pandemic
- Alien Invasion

Do not neglect medications when it comes to your bug-out bag or safe house, but be warned that a lot of medicines can become very dangerous if consumed after their sell-by-date.

Think about what would happen if someone collapsed of a heart attack while you walk to work in the morning. What would happen? Someone would call an ambulance and maybe another person might hold the casualties hand while a group of people gather to watch. Only by the quick actions of the paramedics does the casualty stand any possible chance of survival. If you and your group were on your own and someone had a heart attack what would you do? Do you know CPR? Yes, you've seen it on TV but would you know exactly what to do? Avail of the free training available through Civil Defence organisations. Even if the disaster that you are preparing for does not unfold at least you would be able to potentially save the next person that collapses on the way to work.

Mental Health

If you do not actively strive to maintain your mental health or general outlook during an emergency you will not survive for very long. It doesn't matter how many supplies you have or how well you have prepared, letting yourself succumb to fear, anxiety and self-doubt are as dangerous to you as the disaster itself.

Having a full mental breakdown during a disaster can be easily avoided by keeping your brain active with positive, uplifting thoughts on a daily basis. The S.A.S. (British special forces) are thought to enter any mission on enemy territory with the mindset of "*expect the worst, everything else is a bonus*". Let's imagine for a minute that they go on these missions with the exact opposite mindset. If they are expecting the best and something small goes wrong, then already their minds believe that things **will** go wrong. This will eventually cascade into a long list of things going wrong.

It will become necessary during an emergency to keep track of the days of the week, the date and time of day. This is usually the first thing that you could lose track of but it is also one of the most dangerous things that can easily sap your energy, willingness to survive and mental processing capacity. Keep a journal, with up-to-date calendars that span the next 10 years. Write in your journal every day, about where you've been, what potential food or water supplies you have passed along the way and your general mood.

Maintain a daily routine. We are creatures of habit and actively engaging in any routine behaviour can help to keep us centred and on track. Don't neglect the simple daily routines such as brushing your teeth in the morning and night. Take your deck of cards out of your bug-out-bag and play a game. Even a simple game of *solitaire*, if you are on your own, can help build up your spirits. Keeping yourself warm and comfortable also goes a long way to boosting your mental health. Gaining a boost and keeping it is not about one single herculean task that keeps your mood in check for a day, week or month. It is about doing a series of small things during the day, every day.

Maintaining your general hygiene goes a long way to boosting your mood. When you are clean you feel lighter, it will be easier to stay warm, and you will feel happier. Whenever possible wash yourself and your clothes. Ensure that your clothes are properly dry before putting them back on as a dose of pneumonia will put a bit of a dampener on your day.

Gratitude

Expressing gratitude is by far the best and most effective way to maintain your mental health, not only during an emergency but also in your normal daily life. It should not be used exclusively but should be used in conjunction with the small steps you are already taking such as; keeping a journal, maintaining your morning and nighttime routines and playing games.

Be grateful for everything you have. You could start each day by feeling grateful for being alive or being grateful that you have survived when so many others have potentially perished. Did you sleep in a tent last night? Be grateful that you have a tent to sleep in. Are you away from the immediate danger zone? Be grateful for that.

Every day, spend at least 10 minutes writing in your journal, a list of things you are grateful for. The more feelings of gratitude you have the more things will just seem to feel better. Feeling better about your situation will give you the boost necessary for ongoing survival.

There is also a scientific reason for feeling grateful for things. When you are looking for things to be grateful for your brain will release a compound into your bloodstream called *Serotonin*. Serotonin plays a key role in maintaining a good mood and outlook towards life in general while also relieving anxiety and increasing levels of happiness. Ecstasy is a common recreational drug that makes people insanely happy. If you have ever taken Ecstasy or seen its effects on a user you will know that it has a profound and very quick effect when it comes to boosting a person's level of happiness and positive outlook towards everyone and everything. The reason for this is that Ecstasy causes a massive and sudden rise in serotonin levels in the body. Many antidepressant drugs function in the same way by chemically changing the system in the brain that releases serotonin. I don't recommend that you take Ecstasy or any other illicit drug during an emergency situation. Simply being grateful for things has the same effect but with the added bonus of keeping you alert and fully aware of your surroundings.

Affirmations

An affirmation is something you say to yourself. If you are on the run and have a small hand mirror spend at least a few minutes looking at your face each morning while reciting affirmations to yourself. You can say anything you like as long as it is positive, gives you a sense of confidence and a drive to continue with surviving.

You can recite things like:

- *"I am strong."*
- *"I am confident."*
- *"I am a winner."*
- *"I am a survivor."*
- *"I can overcome any obstacle."*

It may sound like an unnecessary step but did you know that the U.S. Marines teach their new recruits how to use affirmations every day? They are shown an example of a soldier who did not recite affirmations against a soldier who did. They show how all test scores for physical fitness and marksmanship are a lot higher in the soldier who recited affirmations to himself each day. If it's good enough for the U.S. Marines it is good enough for you.

Make sure you recite your affirmations each morning and at night. If you are struggling to march a long distance and feel like giving up just recite your affirmations to yourself and truly believe the words you are saying.

Post-Traumatic Stress Disorder

Post-Traumatic Stress Disorder, or PTSD for short, will most likely become something that you will not be able to avoid following a disaster. This will depend on what you have witnessed or what kind of traumatic events have unfolded since the beginning of the emergency.

The easiest way to describe the effects of PTSD is if you were ever involved in a car accident. Did you replay the events over and over in your mind? When you did replay the events, did it seem real to you? That action of replaying the events indicates that you are suffering from PTSD brought on by experience a traumatic event.

Remember back to the day you had that car accident. Did you feel fear and danger during the event? Most likely you did not and only felt the panic of the event long after you returned home. This is part of the brain's survival mechanism that is designed to downplay dangerous events so that all resources can be focused on survival only. Unfortunately, this survival mechanism is the thing that can lead to PTSD because it forces you to replay events and feel fear and anxiety long after the event itself.

Playing out the traumatic event can lead to anxiety, panic attacks and a feeling that you won't survive the day. The best way to combat PTSD is to maintain contact with other human beings. Talk things out. If this is not possible and you are surviving on your own it is best if you use gratitude but also incorporate a physical activity into your daily routine, such as; exercising every morning. Heavily exercising will force the brain to release Endorphins which make you feel good.

Travel

Being able to travel during an emergency is vital as you may be in danger where you are or you may need to migrate to areas that can provide supplies. In modern days we tend to take travel for granted. Imagine if your car was to stop working right now and all public travel methods failed at the same time. You have no way of getting a lift and you will need to walk anywhere you want to go. How long would it take you to get to the local shop, your place of work or to a hospital? How long would it take you to get out of the city or town where you live?

Let's say, for example, that you live in Lower Manhattan near Broadway and you need to get to the nearest safe area, maybe Sprain Ridge Park just North of Yonkers. Under normal circumstances, this walk could take you approximately 7.5 hours to complete. It could take a lot longer during an actual emergency. Having the ability to effectively transport yourself out of danger is vital to surviving any emergency situation.

Vehicles

During the following emergencies you should have no problem with any basic vehicle except for maybe long queues at petrol stations:

- Economic Collapse
- Super Volcano
- Asteroid Strike
- Chemical / Biological Warfare
- Global Tsunami
- Planet X
- Global Quake
- Pandemic
- Global Famine

If the emergency faced is **Nuclear War**, **Solar Flare / EMP** or **Alien Invasion**, expect all vehicles to stop working. This will be due to the destruction of computerised components within the vehicle that is critical to its operation. Some vehicles will survive but the vast majority will become useless. It all depends on where the vehicle is parked, the distance of the magnetic field from Earth at the time of the event and the orientation

of the vehicle in relation to the epicentre of the event. If you are faced with any of the above disasters it is best if you make a quick check of your vehicle to see if it turns on. If it doesn't, don't wait around and be prepared to move on foot. Any vehicle from 1950 or older will survive such disasters as they will not be equipped with microelectronic computer equipment.

During the above emergency situations, it may prove impossible to extract fuel from petrol stations as they rely on electrical power to pump the fuel. During other emergencies, you may face long queues at petrol stations or rampant fuel shortages. In this case, it may be possible for you to add larger or additional fuel tanks that can be fitted to most vehicles. This would need to be done in advance as it may not be possible once disaster strikes.

While it may seem advantageous to have a large off-road vehicle with a 5-litre engine capacity you will only succeed in running out of fuel very quickly. The best type of vehicle to have is one with a low cc (engine capacity) but still possesses off-road vehicle characteristics such as four-wheel drive. Where possible get your hands on a diesel powered vehicle as these fuels last longer when stored.

When packing supplies into your vehicle make sure you also take a bicycle for each member of your group as you may need to abandon your vehicle at some stage.

Always keep your vehicle adequately maintained to avoid breakdowns at those times when you need your vehicle the most. Make sure you have a full-sized spare wheel and enough tools to perform repairs on the move.

As you may be packing a very large amount of equipment into your vehicle ensure that you have a trailer hitch and roof rack so you can attach additional cargo carrying equipment.

When on the move it may be possible that you inadvertently drain your vehicle's battery. You may be hold-up for a night and by using interior lights, radios, etc. you find that the vehicle does not turn on in the morning. To counter this you can bring a large solar panel and charging station that hooks onto the car battery, allowing for a partial charge, which may be sufficient to start the vehicle within 30 minutes. The longer you charge the battery, the better.

The best possible vehicle for travel during any disaster is the M35. This is a military 2.5-ton truck that can be bought in the U.S.A. as ex-military stock by any civilian and cost as little as €9,000 (USD$10,000). These trucks are designed to run on almost any fuel source such as; diesel, vegetable oil, kerosene, used motor oil, heating oil, transmission fluid, hydraulic fluid, hemp oil and even alcohol (provided it is very strong). While this truck will only average 10 mpg it makes up for this in its ability to use multiple fuel types.

Fuel

During the following disasters you will not need to worry about the longevity of fuel stocks as the supply, even if disrupted slightly, will be restored relatively quickly:

- Economic Collapse
- Super Volcano
- Chemical / Biological Warfare
- Global Tsunami
- Global Quake
- Pandemic
- Global Famine

If however you are faced with **Nuclear War**, **Asteroid Strike**, **Planet X**, **Solar Flare / EMP** or **Alien Invasion** your chance of getting fuel at a petrol station may become impossible. Some modern day disaster shows on TV would have you believe that vehicles will be running years after the apocalypse has begun, even if fuel is no longer produced on Earth, however stockpiling fuel may not prove worthwhile as all petroleum fuels contain certain preservatives that break down after approximately 1 year. Regular fuel will break down and become useless after 1 year where diesel will last for a few extra months.

Navigation

GPS navigation systems should remain unaffected and fully functional during the following disasters:

- Economic Collapse
- Super Volcano
- Asteroid Strike (depending on strike site)
- Chemical / Biological Warfare
- Global Tsunami
- Global Quake
- Pandemic
- Global Famine

Should you be facing a **Nuclear War**, **Planet X**, **Solar Flare / EMP** or **Alien Invasion** expect all GPS navigation systems to either fail completely or, at the least, be very badly affected and should not be used.

The best way to navigate is by using simple map-reading techniques and familiarity with an area. Do you have a place that you can escape to during an emergency situation? Then take the time to practice your escape plans, utilising as many different routes to your bug-out location as possible. Don't rely on a single route as this may become blocked during an actual emergency.

Have detailed ordinance survey maps of your local area, a good quality compass and learn how to read those maps properly. It is possible that common road signs and markers are removed from roads during a disaster, either purposefully by the government or the military, or by people who need sheet metal road signs for their own needs. It is important that you are able to know where you are at any time so you don't get lost.

Tools

Once you have established a permanent base, away from danger, you will need plenty of tools in order to perform routine maintenance, build extensions, build defences, chop wood, etc.

This large amount of tools may prove difficult to take with you so you may need to establish a base far from your current city or town and stock up on the below list of tools. If you don't already have these tools once disaster strikes you may need to find a hardware store to loot.

It is best if you avoid power tools as these can consume an incredible amount of power. Should you find yourself relying on solar panels or wind generators such tools will drain all of your stored electricity very quickly.

The following list of tools can prove useful:

- Adjustable wrench
- All-in-one oil
- Axe

- Bolt cutters
- Box cutter
- Chisels (various sizes)
- Clamps
- Clawhammer
- Drill bits (various sizes)
- Duct tape
- Engine oil
- Glue
- Hacksaw
- Hand drill
- Hand saw
- Hand-powered grinding wheel
- Pliers (various sizes)
- Scythe
- Shovel
- Sledgehammer
- Small Multi-tool
- Socket wrench
- Spirit level
- Step ladder
- Tape measure
- Two-way radio
- Vice grip pliers
- Wheelbarrow

If you have enough space and resources you should expand this list as much as possible. Strive to stock-up on nails, screws and other useful bits-and-pieces whenever you can.

Should you be facing the following types of disasters it will not be necessary to gather large amounts of tools:

- Chemical / Biological Warfare
- Global Tsunami (except where you intend to rebuild)
- Pandemic

How Long Could It Last

Nuclear War

Event duration: 30 minutes to 12 hours

Lasting effects: up to 200 years

A global thermo-nuclear war will depend on which nations decide to launch their nuclear weapons and how many are launched, and what yields of weapons are launched. The war could end after the first salvo of missiles is launched which would see the war lasting only 30 minutes. However, should a nation decide to launch further attacks the war itself will be over within 12 hours.

The after effects of a nuclear war will stretch far beyond your lifetime with many hardships along the way. It could take up to 200 years for the world to return to a stable, technological level, such as we enjoy today.

Economic Collapse

Event duration: 24-hours

Lasting effects: approximately 10 years

Expect to see massive losses on all international markets within the first 2 hours of this event occurring. While this is going on there will be a scramble by governments to cease all trading in order to protect international trading markets. Expect massive drops in currency values within the next 2 to 3 hours. To compensate for global losses you will see massive price increases in commodities such as oil, gas, silver and gold as panic spreads. By the end of the day, your money will become worthless including all of your personal processions and property. You won't be able to sell anything or buy anything as everything will be worthless.

You may wake up the next morning to find that you have lost your job as manufacturing plants, retail shops and other companies close down in order to protect their finances and inventory from further decline. Expect banks to perform mass repossessions of property, similar to what is happening in Ireland since the economic collapse of 2008. As currencies around the world will now be worthless a new global currency will be introduced eventually, probably within 2 to 4 years, but it will still take a significant amount of time before jobs return and things settle down again.

Super Volcano

Event duration: 24-hours to 1 week

Lasting effects: up to 20 years

The eruption will only last for a maximum of 1 week, with catastrophic destruction occurring to the area surrounding the eruption. If there is no warning of the event expect massive amounts of deaths to occur within the directly affected area of the eruption.

Within a few weeks of the initial eruption expect the days to get darker due to the ash cloud. Crops will begin to fail and things will stay in a tenuous condition for anywhere up to 20 years. By this time the atmosphere will clear up and full food production will return.

Asteroid Strike

Event duration: up to 24-hours

Lasting effects: 20+ years

The effects and timeline of this event will be closely tied to the size, composition, speed, angle of attack and location on Earth where the asteroid strikes. We will most likely have no warning and the impact will be the first indication. If the asteroid hits the sea it will cause massive earthquakes and tsunami waves to sweep across the globe. Those coastal areas not hit by tsunami waves will see massive tidal surges within a few hours of the strike.

A large ash cloud will settle in our atmosphere and obscure the sun for many years, leading to crop failures. It could take up to 10 or more years for this cloud to dissipate but the lasting effects will continue. Expect life on Earth to return to normal after approximately 20 years.

Chemical / Biological Warfare

Event duration: from 1 week to several years

Lasting effects: 1 year to 10 years

As with any war, it is impossible to calculate how long it could last for. Let's assume that this war is among several nations or even a full world war that lasts several years. During this time there are many chemical or biological attacks. If there was a series of small-scale chemical or biological attacks by a terrorist organisation it would be over within a week.

Depending on the agent used and the scale of the attack the particular area that was targeted could be hazardous for 1 year or more. If this event is the result of a full-scale war that lasts several years than many areas around the world would be hazardous, with the situation lasting up to 10 years.

Global Tsunami

Event duration: 1 hour to 24-hours

Lasting effects: 10 years

As we have witnessed during the Indian Ocean tsunami event of 2004, waves that strike many thousands of kilometres away from the epicentre will take several hours to travel this vast distance. Expect large-scale earthquakes that send tsunami waves in all directions. Your country may be hit by a tsunami within 1 hour but will also be hit by all the other tsunamis that occur throughout the day.

Most coastlines contain towns and cities that have built-up over many years to accommodate the fishing industry and tourism. The destruction of these towns and cities will represent a massive loss for the planet and it could take up to 10 years to clear away the damaged areas and begin the rebuilding effort.

Planet X

Event duration: several weeks to several months

Lasting effects: 100+ years

As this event is only speculation it is impossible to predict exactly what would occur and the level of damage done. Even though celestial bodies move at tremendous speeds throughout our Solar System they still have a long way to go, so expect the effects of Planet X to last for up to several months, with gravitational pressures causing our planet to shift on its axis. Expect the presence of Planet X to cause asteroids to be knocked off their current orbits and sent hurtling in many directions, one of which will be directly towards Earth.

The effects of this planet passing through our Solar System could last up to 100 years but may last a lot longer. In short, we will be sent back to the Stone Age. That's if we survive at all.

Solar Flare / E.M.P.

Event duration: several minutes to several days

Lasting effects: 15+ years

Massive EMP events have a habit of knocking entire power grids out of commission within a matter of minutes but not all regions on Earth would be affected. Expect power loss and the destruction of electrical and electronic items to occur over a period of a few days as different regions are exposed.

All electrical items will be destroyed, including those machines in factories that produce electrical items. Even large generators and transformers will be destroyed. It could take up to 10 years before a reliable electrical system returns to your country, with further time needed to return us to the technological age that we currently enjoy.

Global Quake

Event duration: 24-hours to 1 week

Lasting effects: 3+ years

This event will most likely see several massive earthquakes occurring within the first day with aftershocks lasting up to 1 week from the beginning of the event.

As whole towns and cities suffer extreme damage the rescue, clearing and rebuilding efforts could last several years with international aid unlikely to come as each country will be struggling to deal with their own crisis.

Pandemic

Event duration: 1 to 2 years

Lasting effects: none

Expect infections and deaths from a pandemic to continue for a few years as global efforts will begin to shift from mass quarantining to the development of a vaccine. It is most likely that nature will stop the virus in its tracks long before an effective vaccine can be developed. After only a few years this event will be over and those that remain will not contract the virus.

There will be no lasting effects after this event as there will only be mass human deaths and no destruction of buildings, etc. There will be a benefit. Due to the massive amounts of people who die there will be a lot of empty houses, more food and far more possessions that you will be free to claim as your own. This happened after the Bubonic Plague (Black Plague) decimated Europe. People simply moved out of their homes in favour of bigger houses and claimed them as their own.

Global Famine

Event duration: 1+ growing season

Lasting effects: 20+ years

When a single growing season fails to yield enough food to feed us all expect mass deaths due to starvation within 1 month. Further deaths will occur until enough food can be grown.

Depending on how the famine began it could take up to 20 years before food production is at a sustainable level and life as we know it now, returns.

Alien Invasion

Event duration: 24-hours to several months

Lasting effects: 200+ years

This event is impossible to create a timeline of events for but we can hazard a guess based on past wars when a superior force attempted to take over a region from a weaker opponent. The aliens will most likely have already selected their priority targets and will wipe these out within the first day of the assault. The ground war could last for months as the aliens search for, and kill, as many humans as they can. Their objective would most likely be to kill enough humans so that we cannot mount any kind of effective assault force anymore.

For those that survive the attacks and go into hiding the lasting effects will continue for their lifetime. If the aliens ever leave our planet, then we will have a chance to rebuild and recover. It could take anywhere from 200 years to thousands of years for us to fully recover from such an event.

Conclusion

As human beings we live in a world filled with dangers that threaten us on a daily basis but, as a species, we possess a tremendous drive to not only survive but thrive. Every disastrous event that we could face is potentially survivable. In the ancient past, human beings have faced cataclysmic problems and we still managed to come out the other end.

Should disaster strike I hope that you will be one of those who survives. Always maintain your strong survivalist mindset and prepare. My most overwhelming wish for you is that you gather supplies and learn to survive but that you will never have to face a disaster.

It is possible that you will face a disaster and quickly lose all of your supplies. But you won't need them as long as you maintain your survivalist mindset. The strongest people on Earth are able to pick themselves up after being knocked down and begin again from scratch. I know you can do the same if you need to. You are a strong, resourceful human being.

Learn to be independent of any other person or societal system and stand on your own two feet. You can live. You can survive. I believe in you.

I wish you continued survival, good health and a long, productive life.

About Tadhg O'Flaherty

As a computer whizz-kid, Tadhg was naturally inept at writing until he discovered that by utilising the Law of Attraction he was able to seamlessly transition into the field and is now a full-time author with several books currently self-published on Amazon.

Tadhg's second book "Surviving a Realistic Zombie Apocalypse" gained local notoriety within days of publishing and was featured on the front page of the Limerick Leader newspaper, which has a readership of 110,290 and also received airtime on local and national radio.

To find out more, visit Tadhg's website and sign up to the author's mailing list for advanced notice of new releases, promotions and more.

www.tadhgfla.com

Author's Note

Thank you for reading **Prepper's: The Ultimate Guide**. I hope you enjoyed this book. Word-of-mouth is vital for the success of any author. Please consider leaving a review on Amazon. Each review makes all the difference and would be greatly appreciated.

I wish you all the best for the future and **know** that you will thrive in everything you do. What would you do if you knew you couldn't fail ever again? Go and do it, build the life that you want.

Also by Tadhg O'Flaherty

How to Get Over Her in 1 Month: Learn how to rise like a Phoenix from the ashes of a breakup

Surviving a Realistic Zombie Apocalypse

Living Off-Grid

Living a Happy Life

Living a Productive Life

Do You Really Exist?

How to Reprogram Your Subconscious

Surviving Crippling Poverty